INCLUSIVE PROGRAMMING
FOR *MIDDLE* SCHOOL STUDENTS
WITH AUTISM/ASPERGER'S SYNDROME

Topics and Issues for Consideration by Teachers and Parents

Sheila Wagner, M.Ed.

Inclusive Programming for Middle School Students with
Autism/Asperger's Syndrome

All marketing and publishing rights guaranteed to and reserved by

FUTURE HORIZONS INC.

721 W. Abram Street
Arlington, Texas 76013
800-489-0727
817-277-0727
817-277-2270 (fax)
E-mail: info@futurehorizons-autism.com
www.FutureHorizons-autism.com

ISBN 1-885477-84-8

Table of Contents

Editor's Note: Throughout this book masculine pronouns are used. This is done to ensure noun/pronoun number agreement. This is not meant in any way to belittle our female students; in fact, feminine pronouns are substituted liberally throughout the text. The use of a particular gender is arbitrary and the location of a particular pronoun has no bearing on its importance in that location.

Foreword

Are you ready for middle school?

Many parents, teachers and administrators have asked for upper-level inclusion manuals. In this book for the middle school, I will attempt to document suggestions, strategies and lessons learned. I hope it proves helpful to both teachers and parents who face years of educational programming for their students with autism and Asperger's syndrome.

Unlike the elementary school manual, this manual is not designed to set up demonstration programs. Nor can it answer all your questions or solve all your problems, simply because students are more varied at this age range. This is not a "cookie-cutter operation."

I will attempt to present different issues and perspectives in this book. Each must be applied individually, taking into consideration the unique requirements of your student. Remember, there are few experts in this area, least of all me. And I continue to struggle with many of the same issues! I hope we can learn together.

Given that there are several definitions of the term "inclusion" across the nation, you will have to determine for yourself what it means. You will have to do this based on your experience and training, as well as on your students' educational experiences. No single definition can apply to all students, yet one definition may apply to a group of students. As a parent or as a teacher, your knowledge and experience equip you to define, develop and apply inclusion programs that are appropriate for your child or for your students.

Middle school students with autism and Asperger's syndrome are, in my mind (and in the minds of many teachers), the "toughest kids on earth to teach." Just when you think you have worked out all the challenges, they will present still more challenges. Therefore, an inclusion program for one student with this disability may be very different from another student's program.

Having said that, let us embark upon a real adventure in education - that of inclusive education for students in the middle school years. Please remember you can modify anything necessary to improve upon what is stated here, or you can throw it all out in favor of your own, possibly better, programs and ideas.

One last note—portions of this manual may repeat some of the elementary inclusion book since many of the readers will not have the earlier manual. If you have that manual as well, you have my permission to skip over the repetitions! Good luck and happy reading!

Sheila Wagner, M.Ed., July 2001

Dedication

This book is dedicated to:

Tom Wagner

My strongest supporter and my refuge, always there with strong arms and flowers when I've hit the wall, a firm believer in all I do. Without your support, I could not do my job or write this book. Thank you for your continued encouragement, prodding, and unbiased (of course), opinion and for that and much, much more, I dedicate this book to you.

And to:

Matt Wagner

Who, I have no doubt, will also publish his writings. May you follow your dreams and have as much fun writing as I. You are one fantastic son and we adore you!

The Puzzle

The puzzle is incomplete, but I do not fit. My edges are rough, my curves don't match the indentations, my colors are muted (compared to the other pieces), and my "picture" is not quite right. The puzzle is incomplete. But how do I fit? I have searched for other pieces only to find them ill-fitting.

Until. . .

One day, the puzzle-solver found me and smoothed my edges, enhanced my colors, rounded my curves, and put my "picture" into focus. I still don't fit every piece, but each day more and more come together for me. I may never fit every puzzle, but thanks to you, I have found my place in many.

Janice Rehder
Mother of included child with autism

May we all be "puzzle-solvers"

Acronyms, Abbreviations and Short Forms

Before delving into the topic at hand, and to prevent having to spell out each expression every time, a list of common acronyms and abbreviations is provided here to aid the reader's understanding of the material.

AS	Asperger's syndrome
B.D.	Behavior disordered (as in classrooms for behavior disordered students).
CBI.	Community based instruction
C.D.D.	Childhood disintegrative disorder
CWA	Children with autism
DSM-IV	Diagnostic and Statistical Manual, Fourth Edition (American Psychiatric Association), 1994.
EARC	Emory Autism Resource Center, Emory University, Atlanta, Georgia
HFA	High-functioning autism
HS	High school
ICD-10	International Classification Division - 10th edition
IDEA	Individuals with Disabilities Education Act (1997). This is the Federal Law which drives all of special education and is the strongest support that parents and teachers have for designing individual programs for their students or children, and for pursuing the "least restrictive setting" for each child.
IEP	Individual Education Plan (or Program). This is the school document that outlines, specifically, the details of a student's educational program. Each state has its own guidelines and interpretations of IDEA, though the Federal law is the foundation for the entire document.
LD	Learning Disabled (as in students with a learning disability)

MS	Middle School
OT	Occupational Therapy
Para; Parapro; Aide; T.A.	Paraprofessional or Teacher's Assistant
Sp.T.	Speech Therapy
SSTS	Student Support Team
Voc Rehab.	Vocational Rehabilitation

1

Autism In A Nutshell

Autism was first identified as a separate disorder by Leo Kanner in 1943. He described similar features he detected in a small group of children that he had been treating. He called this "autism" after the Greek word "autos" which means "self" because these children were very "self-focused" and self-involved. He described the social isolation, unusual behaviors and lack of communication skills that were exhibited in these children.

Interestingly, Hans Asperger from Austria also detected a difference in development in a collection of children in 1944 and named his subset, "Asperger's Syndrome." But since World War II was underway in 1944, his writings were buried, and Kanner went on to be published first. "Autism," therefore, became the collective term for this disorder. It was not until the late 70's and early 80's that Hans Asperger's writings were re-discovered and published widely, leading to the present-day profile of individuals with AS.

Those seeking a technical diagnostic clarification of this disorder, such as school psychologists, will find "autism" as one of the five subcategories in the chapter called "pervasive developmental disorders" in the Diagnostic and Statistical Manual - IV (American Psychiatric Association, 1994). This is the manual that all psychiatrists and psychologists in the United States use to diagnose psychiatric disorders. This category also includes Rett's syndrome, childhood disintegrative disorder (CDD), pervasive developmental disorder - not otherwise specified (PDD-NOS), and Asperger's Syndrome (AS). Rett's syndrome and childhood disintegrative disorder will not be covered in this description, though their profile is considered "autistic," but is even more severe than autism.

Technically, PDD-NOS is not autism, but is often considered a milder form of autism by both professionals and lay persons. Individuals with PDD-NOS, Rett's and CDD often require similar interventions, some more stringent than those with autism and some less, and because of this will not be outlined here in favor of the more traditional "autism."

Asperger's Syndrome will also be covered in this book. Debate abounds as to whether Asperger's Syndrome is a subset of pervasive developmental disorders, or is just another term for "autism." It is clear that individuals with AS are in the autism spectrum, but in the future we may see changes in the label for those individuals who meet this specific criteria, depending upon current analysis of this disorder.

Although individuals with autism spectrum disorders cover a range in severity and symptoms, all of these disorders cause impairment in the three main categories listed below.

Age of Onset of Development

- Deficits usually noted by 3 years of age. This does not mean that the disorder is always diagnosed prior to 36 months of age, just that the symptoms and characteristics develop before this age. Indeed, many individuals are diagnosed much later, even into adulthood.

- Delay in onset of first words and phrases. Typical children use their first words around 12 months and first phrases by 18-24 months of age.

- Uneven skill development (wide variance between verbal and performance scores and between adaptive functioning domains).

- Delays in cognitive skills. The majority of individuals with autism will fall within moderate to severe range of cognitive functioning, though some fall in the average to gifted range as well. However, since cognitive testing is notoriously inaccurate for these individuals, placement decisions should not be based solely on cognitive test results.

One measure currently circulated among the medical profession is the "Checklist for Autism/PDD in Toddlers," or CHAT (Baron-Cohen, 1996), which may assist in the identification process at a younger age.

Impairment in Social Functioning in the Following Areas

- Understanding social gestures and the nonverbal/social implications; ability to read "body language" of others; using body movements to send social messages.

- Eye contact; gaze aversion; inconsistent; non-reciprocal; over-engagement.

- Social smile; reciprocal; responsive.

- Showing and directing; bringing objects to show others for interest; calling other's attention to objects or activities.

- Sharing/turn-taking; spontaneously; upon request.

- Offering/seeking comfort; running to Mom/Dad when hurt; hugging, patting others when they are hurt or distressed.

- Appropriate use of facial expression; expression matching atmosphere of room/activities/other's emotions; showing excitement, caring, expressing sadness appropriately.

- Consistency of social responses; consistency with family members, strangers, teachers; ability to respond in the same manner appropriately to others, such as teachers.

- Imaginative play; ability to use objects in pretend play, fantasy play, representational or symbolic play.

- Ability to play social games; baby games such as patty cake, peek-a-boo; recess games that go beyond run and chase where there is a reciprocal nature to the responses and initiations.

- Ability to make friends; friendships outside of school; reciprocal nature of friendships; age appropriate friends.

- Ability to judge social situations; understanding differences between public and private behaviors; modulating behaviors according to the dynamics of the social situation.

- Imitative social play; playing follow the leader; emulating someone else.

- Interest in other children; seeking out other children to play; making initiations and responses; asks to have others over to play; interested in other children's interests even when not their own.

- Ability to "read" others non-verbal cues; understanding others "hidden agendas"; knowing instinctively when someone is accepting or rejecting them.

Impairment of Communication Domain in the Following Areas

- Oral language: Fifty percent will use expressive language (Lord, 1997), though with intensive early intervention, this statistic has been raised to 82% (McGee, et al, 1999).

- Echolalia: The two types of echoing are <u>immediate</u> (repeating the sentence they just heard), and <u>delayed</u> echoing (repeating sentences and phrases heard previously, such as from TV—videos, seem to be favorites to echo; what teachers or parents have said at school and home).

- Social "chat": Chatting about the day or minor events; "passing the time" by talking about topics of both individuals' interest.

- Reciprocal language: being able to carry on extensive conversations not of their own choosing; listening, responding, building on topics, taking turns talking.

- Appropriateness of language, including grammar, pronouns, gender, tense, etc; individuals with autism sometimes use neologisms (non-words), idiosyncratic language (unusual ways of describing objects, events or people), or exhibit verbal rituals.

- Imitation of language: Although individuals with autism exhibit echolalia, they often do not imitate social or functional language of others in an appropriate context.

- Pointing to express interest: May not point or use gestures coordinated with speech or eye contact.

- Nodding/head shaking: May not use these gestures or uses them inconsistently or, inappropriately.

- Attention to voice: Voice modulation according to environmental situations may lag or be absent; not using voice to appropriately convey meaning or emotion.

- Comprehension of simple language: Many students have better expressive language than receptive; problems with abstract reasoning and inferential processing; liberal interpretation of spoken or written language.

- Direct gaze and reciprocal gaze: Not using eye contact coordinated with spoken language to convey messages; some may over-focus on people or may exhibit gaze aversion; not turning to look at someone else when spoken to.

Impairment in Range of Interests and Behaviors

- Circumscribed interests: Only showing an intense interest in a small number of activities and not wanting to engage in new activities.

- Unusual preoccupations: Over-focus on very unusual, non-age-appropriate objects or activities, such as an interest in electrical cords, science, anthropology, capital D's, or maps and geography.

- Repetitive use of objects: Repeatedly tapping objects, lining up toys.

- Compulsions/rituals: Running patterns in the house; insistence on certain objects in certain places; rigid bedtime routines.

- Unusual sensory habits or interests: Smelling or tasting objects; hyper- (or hypo) sensitivity to sounds; high threshold for pain; visual inspection of objects.

- Hand/finger mannerisms: Flicking hands in front of face; hand-flapping.

- Other complex mannerisms: Repetitive rocking or bouncing; body tapping; combining motor movements into a set pattern.

- Self-injury: Inflicting pain on themselves through biting, head-banging, scratching, picking at scabs, pulling out hair, etc. Some can be quite harmless and some quite serious. None should be taken lightly.

- Special skills: Some individuals exhibit unusual talent in certain areas, even beyond what typical children who are quite bright would tend to; for example, memorizing telephone book entries, calculating complex math problems, music, art, etc.

Students with autism are not to be feared. Many teachers and administrators become anxious when they first hear about a student with the "big A" in their classroom. This is usually because most information recorded about autistic behavior describes the most severe end of the spectrum. Schools and teachers should not judge a student because of misperceptions and misinformation. It is the parent's and special education teacher's duty to appropriately inform the school and administration about autism, providing more accurate information than what is garnered on television talk and news shows.

Note to Teachers

Students with this disorder should not be seen as someone to shut away, never to be heard from again in general education. Students with autism require love, dedication, a solid teacher and schools with a vision of what the student can be and can learn. A student with autism who progresses beyond the wildest dreams of the teacher and principal can set a school on fire with excitement. These students can be loveable and endearing, surprising in their abilities, and can work harder than thought possible. The time and energy needed to analyze behaviors, functioning levels and programs for a student with autism/AS is well worth the effort.

What Is Asperger's Syndrome?

Many parents of students with autism find out about their child's disability when the child is young. By the time the child reaches middle school-age, the family has usually come to terms with this disorder. That is not always true for families that have children with Asperger's disorder. Often, this child is not diagnosed until middle school. By then the social impairment has become obvious, or it has become apparent that behaviors are different from those of typical peers. As a result, many parents and families who try to understand this disorder of Asperger's may feel anger towards professionals for not diagnosing the condition accurately.

Middle school students with AS usually have a history of diagnostic labels which describe the overt symptoms without identifying the main cause of those symptoms. For example, these students may have been previously labeled as learning disabled, obsessive-compulsive disordered, bi-polar, oppositional-defiant disordered and probably many more. This is not to say that all students labeled with these conditions are students with Asperger's Syndrome. Rather, that many students with AS diagnosis usually have these labels in their records. So when you have a student with a variety of such labels, look deeper and consider referral to someone who can diagnose AS.

Since some families are just now coming to the realization that their middle school child has AS, let's look a little deeper into this confusing disorder.

Asperger's Syndrome is considered a severe disability because it is on the autism spectrum, but these people frequently exhibit much milder symptoms. Keep in mind that individuals with Asperger's Syndrome, like folks with autism, are unique, creative and wonderful individuals who are worth all the effort put into understanding their perspective on life.

With that in mind, you should know that Asperger's Syndrome is also considered a sub-category of pervasive developmental disorder in the DSM-IV. There is much debate regarding AS and how it relates to the core features of autism. The main features of this disorder are as follows:

Communication

- No clinically significant delay for developmental milestones in language: First words and first phrases are established before 36 months of age. This does not mean that the student has no problems with functional or pragmatic language. Students with AS often are perseverative with topics, lack understanding of how to use language in sophisticated ways, have difficulties with carrying on conversations and do not coordinate their oral language with non-verbal gestures or body language.

- Unusual vocal tones: Sometimes a monotone or nasal quality.

- Difficulties with voice modulation and showing appropriate emotion in tone.

- Difficulty with reading and understanding facial expressions and body language during conversations.

- Failure to pick up on "social agendas" embedded in conversations.

- May not coordinate their eye gaze with language or mimic the emotions of others in their own facial effect.

- Difficulty with facial expression, eye to eye gaze, body posture, gestures (some are over-dramatic).

- Difficulties with understanding abstract concepts in language; interpret language literally.

Socialization

- Difficulty with peer relationships. Middle school students with AS often know that they are different from other students but do not understand why, nor do they know how to change their behavior to conform to the typical peer's expectations.

- When seeking out friends, an AS student may feel comfortable playing with much younger children. For example, a high schooler will prefer playing with elementary school children instead of with his own peers.

- Lack of spontaneous sharing of appropriate interests or achievements with others; lack of showing, bringing or pointing out activities that might be of interest to others; wants to share own areas of interest exclusively.

- Lack of social and emotional reciprocity. Though some adults with AS who are better able to explain their own disorder state that this is not true, they may demonstrate social and emotional reciprocity differently than other individuals.

Behaviors

- Restricted and repetitive behaviors in interests and activities.

- All-encompassing preoccupation with one or more topics, such as dinosaurs, maps, math concepts, or computers, etc. This area needs to be explored extensively to turn this preoccupation into a real strength for this student's life.

- Inflexible adherence to routines and rituals. This rigidity often gets the AS student into difficulties with teachers. If they don't understand the normal pattern of their day as orchestrated by the teacher, they may very well orchestrate it to their own liking, which will put them at odds with the teacher.

- Stereotyped and repetitive motor movements, e.g., hand flapping, toe-walking, and rocking in their desk or chair, or complex whole-body movements.

- Awkward gross motor movements leading to an odd gait; inability to keep up with typical peers in PE, thereby usually ending up hating team sports.

- Fine motor difficulties leading to poor penmanship and low motivation for writing.

- Motor delays, especially fine motor delays, are sometimes at the root of low motivation for school. Many middle schoolers with AS drop out of school entirely because they cannot tolerate the amount of work being asked of them.

- Persistent preoccupation with parts or objects; e.g., some may carry around favored toys or objects which may interfere with academic tasks.

- Tremendous potential because of their high intelligence quotients, but low adaptive coping skills. This, coupled with frustrations over routines and time constraints in school, sometimes results in outbursts of behavior.

- Outbursts of behavior can range from very mild, e.g., crying, wandering away from the activity, to extreme aggression against themselves or others.

- Occasional high anxiety level. Some students with AS will be able to "hold it together" all through the school day, only to fall apart when they get home, leading to immense frustration on the part of the parent, and disbelief on the part of the teacher, since "they are doing so well at school."

Cognitive

- No significant cognitive delays are noted. Students with AS will have cognitive functioning in the average to above-average ranges, though because of other aspects of their disorder may still not test well. This can lead to inaccurate results on standardized tests. Therefore it is not unusual to see an AS student have IQ results that place them in the below-average ranges. If AS is suspected and cognitive testing does not warrant this diagnosis, repeat testing may be necessary to better evaluate the student's functioning.

- Uneven skill profile. Many AS students will have large splits between verbal and performance on standardized testing but this is not a marker for AS. Because some have this split, you may find the AS student in learning disabled (LD) classrooms. Conversely, teachers often assume that the AS student is just as gifted in all areas of functioning as he is in his particular area of strength. This leads the AS student to multiple frustrations as he tries desperately to keep up with the core curriculum. When he fails miserably, teachers become confused and angry with him. This, factored with fine motor problems, is the cause of low motivation for academics, outbursts of behavior, school phobia, and dropping out of school entirely. Middle schoolers with AS are often home-schooled because of these two factors.

- High academic abilities in some areas. This is mentioned a second time because it is very important and should not be lost in the uneven skill profile mentioned above. AS students often have a real gift in one or two particular areas which qualify them for gifted classes. Some survive beautifully in gifted classes. Others have the ability and would like to survive there, but sometimes gifted teachers have the belief that if they are in that class, they should be able to do everything that the other students do. The student can't always do that. Students with AS may still require some modifications in the gifted class, such as reduced class assignment, computer word processor to compensate for fine motor difficulty, or re-phrasing instruction to reduce abstract concepts.

In short, the AS student can be quite different than the typical student, as well as different from other students with classical profiles of autism. Their enthusiasm for their own areas of interest has earned them the title "little professors," as indeed, they may actually know more about their favorite subject than most professors. These are the children who may, at age five, check out books from the library such as encyclopedias, highly technical mechanical books and other books of adult-oriented reference information. One six-year-old child, after answering questions about toys, playmates, and favorite games, patiently withstood all of the questions and finally said, "Yes, they are nice, but let me tell you about the motors on my leaf blowers." Unfortunately, other six-year-old children are not interested in leaf blower motors and want to play with regular toys and games.

In middle school, the fact that other same-age children are not interested in younger-aged cartoons means that this student will remain isolated. The child with AS often does not have true friends, best friends, or even a group of friends to which they gravitate. Marks, et al states:

Although students with Asperger's Syndrome, particularly those at the secondary level, may appear to avoid social interactions, there is enough evidence to support the idea that many of these students may be interested, but shy away because they lack the skills.

They may want to interact with other students and share interests, but after approaching the groups and talking about leaf blowers or other perseverative interests, the other students "run away" to engage in more appropriate, age-level games. The child with AS is left upset, crying and confused. Eventually, he stops trying to interact.

The middle schooler with AS has usually figured out that he does not have friends and may stop trying to acquire them. He may exhibit his anger verbally, further alienating peers. Social unawareness may also mean that he does not pay particular attention to dress and grooming, leading to disarray in clothing and socially unacceptable habits (for example, picking noses, adjusting private areas of the body, or even placing his hands inside his pants). At the middle school, where typical students are extremely aware of social norms, these behaviors leave the student with AS wide open for teasing and victimization, furthering the frustration and loneliness that he faces daily. Teachers and parents need to take this middle schooler in hand and conduct direct social skills instruction as to what is acceptable in public and what is not, and this must be continuous instruction throughout the school years. Role modeling, demonstration, self-analysis through videotaping and other methods can help this student understand the social norms of society!

Adults with AS often feel as if they are an alien race on earth, faced with a daily struggle to fit into society. They view themselves as very different from "NT's," or neuro-typicals (typical people). Many adults with AS are now speaking out about their disability, and telling the world what it is like to live with this disorder. The wise teacher will seek out opportunities to hear individuals with this disorder so that she may better understand her students.

The following is a classic example of a student with AS. Care should be taken by teachers in interpreting this profile so that they do not become caught up only in the areas of high-ability children. The deficits are equally important. The graph depicts a 13-year-old student who has wonderfully expressive language, much lower receptive language (leading to comprehension problems), delayed social skills, higher domestic skills, very high academic areas (though not in math), and delayed fine and gross motor abilities. These scores are taken from the Vineland Adaptive Behavior Scales (Sparrow, et al., 1984) and cognitive test results. Teachers often see the high performance areas, above age-level and believe that the student should perform at that same high level across the board.

Teachers then become frustrated and angry when the student doesn't. Study the graph to see a true profile of someone with AS and recognize where they will require services and modifications.

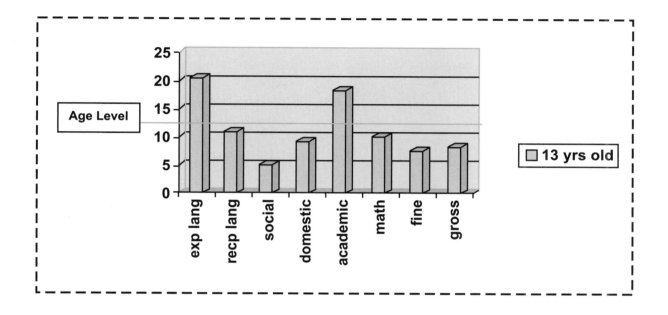

2

Inclusion Discussion

A. Introduction to Middle School

As our students age through inclusive elementary settings, many parents and teachers face the middle school experience with much trepidation. They worry, with good reason, about how their child or student with autism or AS will survive a new and different environment. Middle school is different in almost every aspect from elementary school. Teaching philosophies can also be quite different. Regular middle school teachers often view their role as one to "shape the student up" so that he can face the realities of high school, including academic challenges.

Regular education students, as well as students with autism, suddenly experience less "mothering" or "nurturing" teachers. Students with higher cognitive abilities face an alarming amount of fast paced independent work and a great demand for organizational skills. Middle school students with autism often fail at inclusion because they are assumed to have higher abilities than demonstrated, and therefore do not receive the supports, pre-teaching, or planning that is warranted.

Students with AS often face two dilemmas:

1. They "slip through the cracks" socially, remaining isolated and lonely, or
2. They are placed back into special education classes because they sometimes have difficulty conforming to expected levels of academic output or behavior, or because they are not motivated to perform.

Middle school also poses tremendous challenges involving the typical students in an inclusive program. Typical students are often much less enthusiastic about helping another student in need unless expressly solicited and fostered. At this age, it seems as if the typical student's own self-image is formed by both their friends and their enemies, all of which can change daily.

Human development plays a part, too. At this time middle school students go through hormone surges, which can trigger emotional storms in the best of children. Scales (1991) states:

> *. . . many of our popular depictions of young adolescents leave the impression that the majority is at serious risk of school failure, juvenile delinquency, adolescent pregnancy, and other woes. This is not the case. Developmentally, about 80% of young people do not experience a turbulent early adolescence, and that reality is emphasized. Undeniably, however, all the trends point to a growing number and proportion of young adolescents who are in fact at high risk of being under-prepared and unsuccessful in the modern social and economic world (p. 3).*

The Internet-based National Middle School Association Research Summary # 5 goes on to say, "These growing numbers of at-risk students accentuate the importance of helping young adolescents form coping strategies, a positive self-esteem, and a social support system." For students with autism or Asperger's Syndrome who do not understand how to use coping skills, this can be a very difficult time if they receive no instructions in these important areas.

Educators and parents facing the middle school years should not lose heart, however. Middle school can be a very rewarding time. Students will acquire life skills and knowledge, gain friendships and increased independence when schools and homes work together to design strong, supportive programs that allow for individual preferences and abilities. It is important to understand the positive and negative components of middle school, allowing students to gain from the one, and learn from the other. This is an excellent time to expose our students to some of the rigors of the outside world, allowing them to experience more and more of the outside environment and to push limits, in a safe, controlled environment.

Controlling the environment is crucial at this stage, since middle schoolers do not yet have the power or the wisdom to make adult decisions. Therefore, teacher and parent collaboration is important in designing programs which can challenge children with autism to develop skills they already have, and to learn skills they lack. The partnership should allow them to learn from their achievements as well as from their mistakes. More importantly, it must protect them when outside forces of development, or the world, become overbearing or hurtful. For all the adult-like posturing these children may demonstrate, they are still just children.

Parents and teachers will find middle school topics in this book that should be considered when facing inclusive programming for their students with autism and AS. Nevertheless, they will not be all-encompassing, for it is certain that there are hundreds of topics that could be discussed and analyzed when considering the variability of the individual students with these disorders. I am hopeful, however, that those in this book will be a catalyst for the analysis of the student.

B. Philosophy and Definition of Inclusion

In special education you can find numerous definitions of the term, "inclusion." It has caused great consternation, joy and wonder in many schools, counties, and states across the nation, both for the positive effects seen with the students and for the sometimes negative results that occurred. Debates abound regarding levels of inclusion (Kauffman, 1991, 1993; Fuchs & Fuchs, 1991; and Stainback, Stainback & East, 1994) with little or no real standards established. Individuals in all areas of education have lined up on both sides of this issue, determined to shape children in their own philosophy and ideals. Research articles (Kauffman, J. M., Hallahan, D.P., 1995) warn against the "illusion of support" for all students in inclusive settings, and with good reason. Poorly designed inclusion programs can do great damage to all those concerned. Deno et al., state:

> *Our question is not if inclusion should be the goal schools strive to attain, but how that goal should be attained. We worry that this valued goal will not be attained through rapid, unsystematic adoption of models that may abuse as much as they include. Worse, we fear that our failures, under that banner of inclusion, will lead to a backlash of rejection rather than acceptance of the community school we seek to create.*

To get to the heart of this matter, we must look at the learning pattern of students who have this disorder. Historically, we know students with autism have uneven skill development. They need strategies that require task analysis, repetition of instruction, and demonstration from positive models in some or all domains, depending upon individual needs.

Teaching these students in the natural environment allows for better understanding of needed skills, and the "natural environment" for a school-age child is the wider school system. In short, we can teach our students theory forever. But if we **DO NOT** allow them the day-to-day opportunity to apply that theory, to test it, and to gain faith in the fact that it will work when needed, then we are wasting both their time and ours. If our goal is to train and educate our students with this disability so that they can grow up to function as contributing, independent members of society, then we must enable them to apply what they have learned. The inclusion classroom is the only practical place to do this, and there is no higher goal for parent or teacher than to ensure that our students are immersed in the well-designed inclusion classroom.

While that is a wordy definition of inclusion programming, the bottom line is simple: teaching students with autism/AS in a classroom with typical students, using well-designed inclusion programs that highlight the needs of both disabled and non-disabled students, can offer a wealth of experiences and knowledge for all those involved. Malloy and Malloy write,

> *Responsible inclusion may be the best model for eliminating the debate because it addresses the individual needs of students within the context of permeable boundaries between general and special education (1997).*

A parent's request for inclusion time often forces change in the school district's thinking, causing a re-analysis of available resources. Parents seeking more access to typical students for their child sometimes have an uphill battle. However, teachers and schools can "re-ground" themselves in the ultimate reasons that we educate children, simply by talking to parents. Creating a philosophy of inclusion is not difficult when you ask parents, although schools will want to see that it is backed by research, too. Articles and textbooks, which support this style of teaching, can be found in the reference and resources list at the back of this book.

Most parents want to share their dreams and long-term goals for their own children with the school system, including their hopes for the future when the child graduates from high school and enters adulthood. The hopes and dreams usually center on basic concepts, including that the child:

1. is able to fit into society as best he can;
2. be as independent as possible, including having a stable living arrangement;
3. have friends (including the possibility of getting married);
4. hold a competitive job;
5. be happy.

It would be very unusual, indeed, for parents to request at their child's IEP that "I want you to try as hard as you can to teach my child to be house-bound and segregated from society." Teachers would also never say, "I really want my student to learn as much as he can so that he will be eligible for an institution upon graduation."

No, (thankfully!) the entire educational system is geared toward teaching a student to be as full a member of society as possible. Still, the IEP is often written for the school and not for the student. In the process of determining inclusive settings, parents' hopes and dreams for the child are often not considered. Rather, the decision regarding placement for students with autism is made dependent upon what services are available within the school district and upon the level of training received in inclusive programming.

Today, individuals with autism face a changing society, much different than it was fifty or a hundred years ago. In the past the initial response to persons who experienced a severe disability was to keep them hidden, or to place them in massive public settings (institutions) which "took care" of them. Though that philosophy has certainly changed for the better, support systems for assisting families are not sufficient to help families take care of the child. Anyone watching federal or state funding for social programs quickly realizes that budgets have been cut and service agencies designed to support families are struggling to provide all that is needed for individuals with handicaps.

In today's society everyone, individuals with disabilities included, must be able to function in a world that expects independence. Inclusion in society is expected. We must face this issue in our schools quickly in order to help students with disabilities achieve independence and entrance into the community. Thus they can fulfill their dreams, as well as the dreams of their parents and teachers.

Yet students with autism/AS constitute severe challenges to the educational system. They are among the toughest students to program for, and schools are currently under siege by a variety of therapies and philosophies when designing programs for these students. Parents are not aligned along one course only – some want inclusion, some want a combination of programs, and still others want total specialized teaching in classrooms distant from the mainstream of education.

This makes it tough for schools. Most school administrators desperately want to do what is right for the students, but find their hands tied in a number of ways when faced with varying viewpoints of educational programming and limited funds. Remember – inclusion is just one style of programming and it may not be for every student – it is up to the IEP team to make this decision. It is therefore not enough in today's society for parents to assume schools will provide everything.

Parents must be a part of the solution as well. Inclusion philosophy and programming, if determined to be the best program for a particular student, must be embraced by everyone involved with a student, across all settings, for it to be successful. Parents can do much to support the teachers, principals and administrators when implementing an inclusion program.

Inclusion programming in middle school, if conducted correctly and conscientiously, is definitely not easy. In fact, for students with autism it can be extremely difficult, requiring much time and effort on everyone's part. Therefore, do not attempt inclusion programming unless an understanding of the term "inclusion" and all of the necessary components has been established and ground rules set.

It is clear that more than just rhetoric is required to achieve the lofty goal of inclusion at this age. Cooperation and collaboration to the highest degree will be necessary by teachers who have a vision of what can be. Schools must seek expertise and visionaries to help change philosophies that have entrenched, segregated, and contained students with autism. This will not happen overnight, nor will it happen easily. Many components are essential to making the necessary changes. Those components are outlined in the second portion of this chapter. **ALL** components are necessary and none are expendable. Elimination of any one component means lack of quality, lack of duration, and a dilution of effect.

C. Necessary Components

The necessary components for a solid inclusion program were first outlined by this author for the elementary ages (Wagner, S., 1999). These same components are still necessary for success in middle school and will be outlined here and described for this age range. The IEP team should consider the following components when including a middle school student with autism/AS into general classrooms.

Administrative support

Lack of administrative support poses many barriers to inclusion programming in middle school. Without the principal's or special education director's support, the longevity of the program will be questionable. Teachers conducting inclusion programming are indispensable and need to know that their supervisors support them, that they will be flexible when needed, and that they will offer resources and support for their teaching methods. Administrators should make a point of routinely visiting the classroom. They should get to know and understand the child so that they will be able to enjoy the student's progress. A personal attachment to the students helps immensely.

Teachers can always tell the principal how much the child is progressing. But unless administrators actually see it, they may not believe it. Worse, they may dismiss it as unimportant. In one school, for example, an assistant principal used every opportunity to cast doubt on the inclusion project, complained about the students behavior, and in general, felt that students with autism did not belong in regular education classes. However, once this administrator was invited into the classroom to observe and spend some time with the students, she realized what wonderful children they truly were, and began to watch for progress and was overjoyed when it came! This administrator fought to retain the children in inclusive settings and became a true asset to the program.

Flexibility and vision on the part of the administrator are also important. Students with autism or AS require understanding and support from the administration while the chaos (usually in the beginning of the year) is sorted out.

Students with AS often pose challenges to the administration because of behavior problems and unusual profiles. At this age, behaviors can sometimes be more severe than in the elementary ages. Unless the principal is able to see beyond these issues, the student is often pulled from the regular classrooms and returned to the self-contained class quickly, after the first few behavioral outbursts.

Sometimes, administrators become very frustrated with the day-to-day problem solving and, if aggression is exhibited, may use the "easy out" by suspending the student, or even calling in the police over behaviors that have been exhibited. Some administrators have even filed charges to rid their school of the problem child. Although students must certainly follow the law, students with AS are not typical "conduct disordered" or "emotionally handicapped" students and do not fully understand the consequences of their behavior. Unfortunately, the entire scenario of police, handcuffs, and jail can be extremely traumatic for a student with AS, and he may never recover. Understanding and compassion from the administration is called for, as well as strict and consistent positive behavior programming to help the student with autism or AS adopt appropriate behaviors which can sustain him/her through life (see the behavior section in this book). Administrators who perceive the student as someone who needs retraining and who must have their support, will then focus on the future for this child, and help sustain the program through the hard times.

Teacher training

Teachers attempting inclusion programming for students with autism-related disorders certainly need basic training in autism, but that is seldom enough. McGinnis (1982) notes that students who have autism do not constitute a homogeneous group, but vary widely from one individual to another. Teachers may learn the basic information about autism/AS from a full day workshop and become inspired, excited, and energized. The effects of the workshop quickly disappear, however, when the teacher hits the first rough time. For example, when faced with behaviors she hasn't seen or heard of before, or when faced with a profile of autism not covered in the workshop, the teacher's idealism may well disappear. Also, student resistance to any and all of her tried-and-true techniques may send the teacher scurrying to find solutions.

Inclusion teachers need continuous support throughout the year by someone experienced in the full range of autism. These more experienced mentors can help the inclusion teacher analyze behaviors, teach new strategies and techniques, and hold their hands when the going gets tough. Weekly or bi-weekly visits or training sessions from an experienced behavior/inclusion specialist are fine; monthly visits are a bare minimum. If local support isn't available for training, administrators should look elsewhere. According to Malloy,

> *Collaboration and interactions between teachers and university researchers as well as school administrators should also be a part of the inquiry and problem solving process. (Malloy, W., Malloy, C., 1997).*

Students with autism/AS often have complex profiles across the spectrum. Consequently, the lessons learned when dealing with one student cannot necessarily be used on the next student with autism. In order to maintain an inclusion program, schools must continually retrain teachers for new students. This gives schools added concerns regarding funding, and leads to hesitation in embracing this style of teaching. Therefore, when considering inclusive philosophies, dozens of reasons to reject this style of programming can be found. Parents, however, can provide hundreds of reasons for the reverse.

To be sufficient for a foundation of knowledge to include children with autism, teacher training sessions should include the following topics:

- Characteristics of autism/AS (full spectrum)

- Behavioral strategies. Emphasis on positive programs for middle school, but also addressing natural consequences of the environment and society, especially for AS students (please see the section addressing characteristics of AS for reasons for this statement). [p. 20]

- **Differential Reinforcement of Other/Alternative/Incompatible Behaviors (DRO,DRA,DRI)**

- Social Skills
    - Assessment; IEP objectives; how to imbed social skills into curriculum
    - Peer programming/peer reinforcement
    - Academic modifications/accommodations

- Environmental modifications/accommodations
    - Teaching strategies
    - Redirection methods
    - Direct instruction methods
    - Peer teaching/peer programming

- Transition issues

- Paraprofessional support: levels of coverage and methods of support/fading of support

- Related services (OT, speech, PT)

- Communication strategies
  - Development of oral language
  - How to elicit oral language
  - Augmentative systems
  - In-class services versus pull-out therapy

- Collaboration (Special Ed-to-Regular Ed; School-to-Home)
  - Daily, weekly, monthly information exchanges
  - Collaboration between school/community therapists

- Medication effects with students with autism/AS
  - Medication monitoring
  - Collaboration between home/school/physician

Most teachers receive training on all of these subjects in routine staff development sessions. However, the emphasis in routine training sessions is rarely on a practical level for an inclusion program, especially when considering the middle school setting. An inclusion classroom is completely different from a self-contained setting. Training on all of these subjects must be done with the general classroom in mind if inclusion is to be considered for students with this disorder.

Parents as True Team Members

Parents should be viewed as the real experts on the student and true team members in educating the student. The teacher will find an exceptionally strong resource in the student's parents. This information is easily accessible if only teachers will pursue it. Most parents want to provide input and receive on-going information regarding what the child is taught at school. Parents have been teaching the child a lot longer than the teacher (especially since this is now a middle school student), and know more than most about the problems of generalization of skills. That was one of the very first lessons they learned. Anyone who has ever toilet trained a small child with autism knows this very well.

Therefore, parents should be consulted whenever possible to provide suggestions, clues to behavior, and information on the child. Parents should be provided with daily, weekly and monthly updates on their child. This is the best way to analyze generalization of skills and to make informed decisions regarding goals, objectives, and behaviors. Parents should be involved as true team members throughout the year, not just at the IEP meetings.

Parents, for their part, should not assume there are negative motives behind the request for information, i.e., "My child's teacher doesn't know what she's doing because she called today to ask for my help in solving my son's behavior problem! It sounds like she doesn't know how to do her job!"

Be happy that the teacher is wise enough to ask for your opinion! Parents have a wealth of information to share. Please take this opportunity to do so. No one has all the answers with this disability.

Inclusion Facilitator or Manager

School systems which include many students with autism in general education classes have learned the value of having a member of their teaching staff monitor and be responsible for the inclusion students' programs. A facilitator or manager who rotates routinely through the classrooms or schools that house the inclusive students can offer problem solving techniques and resources to the general education teacher. The inclusion facilitator should be, above all else, a solid teacher with detailed knowledge and expertise in the areas of behavioral programming, the disability of autism, and methods and strategies for academic remediation. She should also know how to address the area of social skills in the regular education setting.

Flexibility is also essential, for the facilitator will be presented with any number of situations on a daily basis; each must be analyzed and solved. Of course, unless a school district has many students with autism in general education settings (i.e., 15 - 20), it is not economically feasible for the school to have this non-classroom teacher. This makes it difficult for small districts with one or two students with autism in general education settings to provide the appropriate support to those teachers in regular education classrooms. The IEP holder, usually the self-contained teacher, will need to assume this role; however, it will be a difficult proposition for her to manage in addition to her students.

The inclusion facilitator also needs an extensive knowledge base. In well-developed programs (Wagner, S. 1999) the inclusion facilitator receives continuous in-depth training for as long as two years. Most schools, however, do not have the luxury of grant funding to subsidize inclusion programs. They must look to other sources when considering support for their teachers. They should look to foundations or local funding sources that can enter a partnership (many schools are directly linked to businesses) to develop the funding for on-going training packages.

So how can regular education teachers in small school districts receive the continuous support for an inclusion program when they have neither a full-time facilitator nor a therapist assigned to watch over them, nor do they have grant funding to establish a larger program? For every included student, middle schools will have numerous teachers who require support. Administrators must be creative and employ a number of methods such as:

- Implementing teacher-mentoring programs, pairing new teachers with the previous year's teachers of the inclusion students.

- Hosting staff development meetings after school for the teachers to share information and concerns, and solve current problems.

- Sending teachers to conferences on various topics of autism education.

- Arranging weekly meetings with the county behavior therapist.

- Having the special education director visit the classroom more frequently.

- Conducting in-depth data collection on various behaviors and objectives (which should be going on anyway) to track performance.

- Encouraging parent input to the program.

- Periodically pairing general education classrooms (one inclusion classroom and one non-inclusion classroom) for 20 - 30 minutes (provide down-time, video watching, group projects, forums, etc.), thereby allowing one teacher time to hold a collaborative meeting with the special education director while the other teacher supervises the combined classroom. The teachers take turns being host, so that the other teacher can conduct a meeting, do research, meet with parents or prepare materials for her classroom.

- Pair two homerooms prior to school starting to allow teachers to listen to a guest lecturer. The lecture is then taped for the other teachers.

Continuing support of the inclusion teacher, and therefore the student, is crucial to the success of any inclusion program. Without it, many teachers and schools struggle to conduct this new style of teaching in the regular education setting. An inclusion facilitator or manager is ideal; without these people providing continuous support regular teachers can become frustrated, burned out and form negative opinions of both the student and the philosophy of inclusion. These problems are the result of the multiple and complex issues presented by a student with autism, especially at the middle school level. Further details of the program manager's duties will be discussed in Chapter 8.

Teacher Collaboration

Both regular and special education teachers need time to share information with other team members. This is never truer than in middle school. Parents and administrators should not expect teachers to do their jobs to the fullest without knowledge of the other components of the student's program and how the various components interact. Also, the general education teacher needs to understand what objectives, cues, strategies and methods are used with the student in other areas of programming. This cross-learning increases the likelihood of generalizing the skills across settings.

Often, the regular education teacher hasn't a clue as to what other specialists (occupational therapist, music teacher, P.E. teacher, community therapists, etc.) are teaching the child. Lack of collaboration among these professionals may cause the student to end up with a number of varied but unrelated programs. While this is a common problem in any inclusion program, it is especially damaging to students with autism, since the need for collaboration at this age is crucial for addressing generalization of skills. Too many teachers are "in the dark" when it comes to related services objectives. Also, many parents provide community therapies for their child to supplement the school program, but few community or school therapists ever exchange information on a routine basis.

Forms provided by the special education teacher to other teachers of the student can be very helpful to fostering and maintaining the necessary information exchanges. Teachers are encouraged to review the work of colleagues in the field for information on collaboration, including forms that can prove helpful to the program. This section will be expanded upon in Chapter 8.

Proximity to typical peers

The issue of proximity to typical peers has taken on new meaning for most school districts. Informed parents are now demanding that school systems provide this new style of teaching for their children, and school systems are responding in a number of ways. Some embrace the philosophy, some refuse directly and inflexibly, some are willing to attempt it half-heartedly, and some are determined to take the issue to the courts. Some schools "give in" to the parents by throwing the student with special needs into regular education classes without the support or training necessary to make the program a success, and when the program fails state categorically that "inclusion doesn't work."

Proximity alone is not, in this author's opinion, "inclusion." It is the first step only, since proximity to typically developing students must be available before the teacher can attempt the inclusion steps. It does not mean that the student with autism will automatically learn. Many times and in many schools, proximity to typical students is impossible to achieve, either because the school is segregated from general education schools, or because behaviors are so aberrant that the student would cause significant harm to himself or others if placed in a general education class. (If this is the case and behavior is the main reason for the segregation, then a full behavior analysis is warranted in the hopes that the student can be returned to the general education school.) Without access to typical students, individuals with autism will lack the opportunity to practice and generalize skills in a natural setting. The ultimate question then, is this:

> *If teachers cannot help the student with autism generalize and practice the necessary skills (for which we have been, supposedly, expressly trained), are parents going to be any more successful when their child reaches age 21?*

There is nothing magical about the twenty-first birthday. Students do not automatically receive survival skills with their special education diploma from the school system. We cannot teach students with autism in isolation for 17 years and then expect them to survive in a typical world. Looking at statistics, we know this doesn't work, and the result has been that parents spend a lifetime struggling with their home-bound adult child.

"Inclusion" therefore, has taken on a new meaning for the neighborhood school, and for the federal government. Although in the U.S., the Individuals with Disabilities Education Act (IDEA, 1997) has many initiatives for inclusive programming, it does not "mandate" that every child with a disability be forced into a general education classroom. It does mandate, however, that the Individual Education Program (IEP) team must first consider the least restrictive environment when programming for special needs students. That means they must START with regular education, not END with it when considering placement. Instead of having to explain how students can "earn" their way into these classes, reasons for placement out of general education classes must be explained.

This access to peers must be an option to all students regardless of disability. However, profiles of students with autism are quite varied, and even with access to typical students, each student's program must be specifically designed around that student's profile.

Data Collection

Data collection throughout an inclusion program is the only way teachers and parents can truly assess progress. Many parents and teachers get very excited about the progress and anecdotal reports they get from their child's teachers. This progress must be reflected in the daily or weekly collection of data for the IEP objectives if there is any hope of making informed decisions.

Also, many students have behaviors that affect their program. Before changes in programming can be made (for increased or decreased exposure to typical students, levels of support, etc.), data collection must be taken to substantiate the decisions. Systematic data collection is especially important for students at this age who transition between so many classes each day and may have a number of teachers who do not communicate very often. Without systematic data collection, accountability can be lost and programming can become suspect.

Data collection forms can be developed by the special education teacher that will help the inclusion teachers track IEP objectives on a daily or weekly basis. But the special education teacher can make the data collection much more manageable for the inclusion teachers. One method is to analyze the student's scheduled classes and then choose certain objectives for analysis. For example, only one or two objectives may be designated for each class.

Over the course of the day, the various teachers, through this type of selection, can address all of the student's IEP objectives. For example, the math teacher can address on-task attention and listening behaviors; the language arts teacher can address vocal tone and comprehension; the PE teacher can address requesting help, sharing and turn-taking and vocal tone, etc.

At the next reporting period, the IEP objectives are rotated. There may be some objectives which all teachers address all the time. Some student-specific objectives may need to be taught and tracked for the whole day. The special education teacher is the best person to make this determination. The rotation of objectives is important since the goal is to generalize the objectives across all teachers. Middle school teachers are often less threatened by a special education student attending their class when they know that they will have to address only a certain number of objectives, rather than the whole IEP.

Data collection is also important for teachers. Teaching is a noble field, but in this litigious world, it is not uncommon for teachers to have to participate in mediation or due process hearings. Without data collection to substantiate decisions, the teacher can be made to feel extremely foolish and unprofessional, to the extent that they may leave teaching. Teaching methods, therefore, should be research-based and consistently documented.

The wise teacher keeps up with her field, and is able to accurately document the progress of her students.

3

Profiles and Characteristics of Middle School Students

A. Profile of the Typically Developing Middle School Student

In order to understand the middle school student with autism or AS, it is important to fully understand the profile of the typical student in this age range. Variations in developmental milestones and maturation rates lead to a very complex child indeed. As outlined by Scales (1991), early adolescence has seven areas that require attention:

1. Positive social interaction with adults and peers
2. Creative expression
3. Competence and achievement
4. Structure and clear limits
5. Physical activity
6. Meaningful participation in families and school
7. Communities, opportunities for self-determination

Adolescents are at the age where they seek approval from adults and peers but don't want anyone to know it. They are at the crossroads between childhood and adulthood, with one foot in each camp. They spend these middle years dancing between these two groups and not being very good at either one.

Middle school students can be physically short, or they can be a 6-foot, 5-inch 13 year-old who is mistaken for the teacher. Differences in height and build can make for many instances of teasing and embarrassment. Students in these grades learn to be "on guard" with certain peers who may tease or victimize them because of perceived differences. This can lead to a level of defensiveness and wariness which can push the child into impulsive or instinctive reactions. Emotional outbursts are the norm rather than the exception. The wise teacher will support the student without seeming to, will offer this support outside the purview of the peers, and will not "rat" on the student to the parents unless there is a strong need.

Middle schoolers are also finding that they can "stretch their wings" and orchestrate their lives to a certain point (and will attempt to do so at every opportunity). But they are not capable of understanding the full, adult ramifications of their actions when things go wrong. Because they often have to face the adverse consequences of their impulsive actions (not looking before they leap), their emotions often swing wildly as they try to explain their way out of situations.

Academic demands are also much higher than in elementary school. The middle school student often feels lost in the larger building with a larger number of teachers, though they are usually excited to be a part of this "grown up school." Middle school teachers have a large impact on the self-esteem of the middle school student. Teachers usually view their jobs as preparing the student for the rigors of high school. Therefore, they often set very strict guidelines for classroom behavior, with little or no room for negotiation. On the one hand, this offers the student the continued structure that they, as a child, still need.

On the other hand, however, the strict structure offered by the teachers often goes head-to-head with the "creative" thinking of the middle school student, creating potential conflict. Middle school teachers take their jobs very seriously, and asking them to change their routines or their style of teaching for one student (be they typical or special need) is sometimes very difficult.

Wigfield & Eccles (1994) noted a decline in adolescent self-esteem during this time, as well as in how students valued school subjects. Competency in subject materials was an area of concern for middle school students facing self-esteem issues. School failure rates are also of concern to parents, teachers and administrators alike since many students face difficulties at this time.

Adolescence can be a wonderful, fulfilling time. It can also be a time of turmoil. Nowhere will you find such enthusiastic students willing to help and support one another. Their boundless energy, creativity and idealism can be tapped for individual, group or school-wide projects. Middle school students fully believe that they can change and improve the world, and no teacher ever wishes to disillusion them.

Teachers find that they must often channel the middle schooler's enthusiasm into areas which will help them grow academically and socially. They must help them get their "feet on the ground" and be ready for the transition to high school. Middle school teachers will almost always say that their job is difficult, but that they wouldn't teach in any other area of education. These teachers are to be commended and reinforced heavily for their understanding and support of the typical student through these very rough years.

B. Profile of the Middle School Student with Autism/AS

Teachers will find many different profiles of students with autism/AS entering middle school.

Middle School Students from Self-Contained Classrooms

One profile involves the students who are coming from self-contained classrooms where they may have been in one classroom with one special education teacher and a small group of students with special needs for all the elementary school years. These students may be verbal or non-verbal (the non-verbal profile is discussed later in this chapter). The verbal student may have either autism or Asperger's Syndrome.

In this setting, your new student may have been exposed to many inappropriate behaviors in the classroom. She may have imitated a number of those behaviors, and as a result, will have created her own, unique behavioral profile. This will pose many challenges when considering a middle school inclusion program.

Any inclusion program considered will have to be carefully developed and implemented slowly. It will have to rely heavily on well-designed behavioral modification systems which bring the autism/AS student's behaviors into line with those expected of typical middle school students.

It will seem as if there is not enough time in the day to provide all that this student will need. To repeat, throwing a student with this profile immediately into a full inclusion program is extremely problematic, though not impossible (never say 100% for anything in this disability). It all depends on the particular characteristics of the social, behavior, and language skills of the student, and of course, the receptivity and expertise of the teachers involved.

Close coordination between home and school will be necessary to identify all of the parent's goals for their child, and decisions must be made as to the level of inclusion, functional skills, and community involvement. As with all students, long-term goals should be the defining factor for this student. Where do parents and teachers see this student when she is 35 or 40 years of age? Keeping an eye focused on the child's adult years can help the team design a program that will encompass all of the necessary components, (e.g., interaction with community, self-help skills, domestic skills, functional academic skills, recreation/leisure skills, etc).

Total or Partially Included Student

In contrast to the preceding, more severe profile, teachers are also likely to encounter a student who comes from a history of total or partial inclusion. They have been taught alongside typical students for all or most of their elementary years. These students will have had many experiences and gained many skills which can ease their inclusion into middle school classes. These include attending skills, expectations for daily work and homework, raising hands when answering or requesting help, knowledge of the usual patterns of school routines and environments, participation in core academics and expected school behaviors.

However, knowledge of these expectations does not always mean compliance. Depending on her particular profile, your student may still have difficulties. It is also highly likely that, to be successful, she will require some academic modification, behavior management programs, reinforcement systems, and possibly a level of paraprofessional support. We hope that this student will be able to help maintain the environment of the regular education classroom so that all students can learn. Keeping up with the core curriculum content (modified or non-modified), social groupings in the classes, being able to form or continue friendships, and continuing to increase independent skills in the natural environment are goals that probably have been worked on in the elementary years. Parents will expect them to continue in the middle school years as well.

If the student is verbal, this middle schooler will likely have increased his skills over the elementary school years. He may still have problems with sophisticated layers of language such as reciprocal conversations, conversational turn-taking, or appropriate topic changing. Abstract concepts will also cause problems. It is best to conduct a full social skills and pragmatic language analysis at least twice a year (three times is better) to identify the areas where this verbal student will need work. Pre-post assessments are necessary for documenting changes, but the mid-term analysis will provide you with time to make corrections and an opportunity to refine objectives.

High-Functioning Verbal Student

The teachers may encounter another profile: a high-functioning, verbal student with autism or AS who has failed in an inclusion program. This student will have had exposure to typical students but experienced many problems: possible inconsistent levels of programming, little teacher training, inappropriate support levels while in the general education class, as well as numerous and erratic outbursts by the student because of this disability. All this results in teacher and parent frustration. This student's behaviors, combined with the results of the poor programming usually precede him and teachers are leery of including them in middle school.

Another profile is that of the autistic student who is very high-functioning and verbal, but also very passive. This child may be able to perform the academic work and has no overtly inappropriate behaviors, but is isolated, has poor interpersonal skills (that may not have been addressed before), possible poor grooming skills, and may not even be diagnosed. He also spends all of his time alone, both in class and during non-structured times. He eats lunch alone, visits the library alone, and rarely talks to anyone. This is a very lonely child.

Non-Verbal and Pronounced Autism Disability

Finally, there is the student who is non-verbal and has a more pronounced autism disability, along with cognitive impairment. In this case, it is imperative that he have a solid communication system which functions across all settings and with all people. Support systems such as symbol-systems communication boards, picture systems, voice-output devices, computer-generated systems and other alternative systems should be well established by now, at least in larger metropolitan areas. If they are not available, contact the speech therapist and immediately begin the process of identifying the best communication system for this particular student so that he will have methods of communicating with teachers and the other students.

Inclusive programming is conducted so that the person with the disability will have ample opportunity to develop social and language skills. If he is non-verbal and has no consistent system, then the student will be very frustrated indeed. High tech devices are fascinating for everyone. Many times, however, the student with autism does not understand or respond to the system for many reasons and therefore won't use them. Devices such as computer voice generators are attractive and exciting, but are fragile and may not be able to stand the rigors of handling by a middle school student.

Middle school students with autism often do not understand that they are different from other students in school. They go about their day believing everyone is exactly like them. This lack of perception makes it harder when teaching the student with autism to "be like his peers" in inclusive settings because he doesn't cue to the social behaviors that teachers want him to emulate. The student may not be aware that what he does sets him apart from his classmates, and so he is not motivated to emulate his typical peers to be "accepted."

This is unlike students with Asperger's Syndrome who often know full well that they are very different from the other students, and may spend much time anguishing over why they are different. Sometimes this leads to performance anxiety with schoolwork, depression over lack of social skills, and frustration with school in general. Sadly, this depression and anger sometimes results in thoughts of suicide, or even suicide attempts. The student's teachers must watch for depression signals and seek help immediately. Close coordination with the parent is a must for this student. Severe depression can start early in the life of a student with AS, even in elementary school years.

The Individuals with Disabilities Education Act (IDEA) states that we must consider the regular education classes first and foremost. Flinging a student with a severe autism profile and history directly into full inclusion on day one of middle school, without (and sometimes even with) massive training and full supports will likely be disastrous. If they have cognitive impairments as well as the severe disability of autism, options for functional and community based instruction (CBI) may be considered. Academic schedules will therefore have to be closely analyzed in order to find times to conduct the inclusive program and still teach necessary functional and community skills if the IEP team wishes.

There are many profiles of students with autism and Asperger's Syndrome in middle school. Only a few are listed here. The importance of recognizing this variety of profiles is that it precludes the use of a standard format for inclusive programming for all students who exhibit this disability, and demonstrates why each detail of the program for each student must be examined over and over again. There is nothing easy in inclusive programming at this age.

C. Where Do We Find Middle School Students with Autism/AS?

If you are a teacher acting as a new facilitator and this is the first time you have looked for the student with autism, it is likely that you will find them languishing in self-contained special education classrooms. The reasons for being in segregated classrooms are many, depending on the school and parents. For example:

- They may have a more severe profile of autism.
- They may have cognitive impairment and cannot stay on grade-level in the core academics.
- The school may not understand or wish to implement inclusive styles of teaching.
- The school may not wish to spend money on the paraprofessional support needed for student success.
- The school may be entrenched in the philosophy of "keep autistic students in contained classrooms because it is easier to control the environment."
- The students' behaviors may be difficult to manage in the general education classrooms.
- The parents may not want their child exposed to teasing or bullying by typical students.
- Other students may be in inclusive settings but they may not have enough general education classrooms for all of the special needs students to have this experience.

- Self-contained classrooms are quieter than general education classes, have lower numbers, and offer more opportunities for individual instruction, including functional skills.
- The teachers have no training and feel ill-equipped to conduct inclusion.
- Regular education teachers refuse to have the students in their classrooms.
- Any of a thousand other reasons . . .

At this stage students with more severe forms of autism, as well as those with severe to moderate cognitive impairment, are often not considered for inclusion or for any access to typical students. They may have very unusual behaviors such as self-stimulation, self-injurious behaviors, aggression towards others or severe delays in overall adaptive functioning. Such students are relegated to the self-contained setting throughout elementary school and the setting is continued in middle school. Further, they may lack solid communication systems or methods to converse with others.

However, you may also find the student with HFA (High-Functioning Autism) in self-contained classrooms because they can't stay on grade level due to their uneven skill profile, or because of outbursts of behaviors. Indeed, many students with AS are found in behavior disordered (BD) classrooms or self-contained learning disabled (LD) classrooms due to behavior alone. Just because they are in self-contained classrooms does not mean that they cannot have access to typical students. It does mean that the teacher must carefully plan and thoroughly analyze any programs for these students.

Keeping such students with autism/AS in inclusive settings at this age is more difficult. Many of the factors that make it difficult to keep HFA students in inclusive settings are outlined and discussed later in this book. Teachers and parents must consider these factors in light of their particular student.

We also find potential inclusion students with AS drifting, unidentified, in regular education classes. They may have no IEP, they may have no clear or formal diagnosis, or they may have truly "fallen through the cracks" because, in spite of their disability, they are able to keep up with their academics well enough to get by in regular education classrooms. They may or may not be labeled as "manipulative" or as "bad kids."

The teacher may also be irritated because she can't figure out the child. Students such as these are finally identified only because their social skills are recognized as different, though not always. They may even slip through until high school or beyond without ever being diagnosed.

Regardless of which profile the teacher is presented, it is to her advantage to fully understand the characteristics of autism/AS and better understand her student's methods of functioning and processing. Without this knowledge, too many teachers form erroneous ideas of why a student is misbehaving. Individuals with autism/AS usually, and quite genuinely, want to please the person making the requests of them. They just do not understand how best to get their own message across, how they feel about the request, or how best to comply with the teacher's demands (and therefore get her to stop asking).

Knowledge of this disorder provides insight into the student's confusion, and gives a better understanding of how best to present information, and how to moderate behavior.

Obviously, there are many difficulties and impediments to inclusive teaching. While the difficulties of inclusive programming in middle school are considerable, do not let them persuade you to automatically rule out access to typical students. Neither should you design a program that is based on services or conditions available in the middle school. You are still a teacher or a parent and you need to design a program for this student.

4

Formation of an Individual Education Plan (IEP)

For those parents whose child has recently received a diagnosis of autism or Asperger's Syndrome, developing an IEP will be an unfamiliar process. Many regular education teachers do not know what an IEP is because traditionally, general education teachers receive little or no training in programming for a special needs student. Your inclusion student may be the first with whom the teacher has been involved. It is not unusual to have a middle or high school student be diagnosed at this time, as many students with milder profiles of autism "slip through the cracks."

This does not mean that the parents or teachers did not understand that something was unusual with the child, just that a formal diagnosis was not conducted and therefore the student didn't require special services. This is also true of a child with Asperger's Syndrome, since many professionals still do not recognize this disorder as separate from someone with learning disabilities, attention deficit/hyperactivity disorder, schizophrenia, oppositional-defiant disorder, conduct disorder or a host of other emotionally-based disorders (see Chapter 1). Many parents, therefore, may be first introduced to an IEP during the middle or high school years.

Many times the AS student is targeted for screening at this middle school age because the social difficulties become an overriding concern and are more noticeable. In the elementary years this was a cute child who had great abilities and unusual social interactions and the child did not have behavioral outbursts, so he may not have been unusual enough to warrant an investigation. In fact, many teachers are often enamored with the AS student in elementary school because he is so cute and knowledgeable. The teacher is not overly concerned that this student would rather interact with the teachers than with other students. However, by the time this student gets to middle school, the social difficulties and academic quirks become overwhelming for the teacher, and the student is no longer "cute" and engaging, but presents difficulties in a number of areas that can no longer be ignored.

If this is a first-time referral, the teacher will refer this child to the Student Support Team (SST). Clear regulations exist that drive the SST process, and the parents must be notified before it begins, and must be asked for permission to refer their child to the SST process.

The SST is a mechanism mandated for all schools by IDEA. Its purpose is to help students remain in regular education. Once parental permission is given, the student is referred to the SST. The school must then set up a team of teachers who will examine the student in light of his academics, behaviors, language and social issues, and offer academic modifications and accommodations to help improve the classroom situation.

At the initial meeting, the SST will set a date to review the results of its recommendations. The recommendations must then be implemented and data collected on results. When the review date arrives, the team will meet to evaluate progress, and can decide to offer more suggestions to the teacher, or refer the student on for a full evaluation.

If the student is referred for a full evaluation and special education services (this may actually come at the first SST meeting if the needs are crucial or if the student is in crisis), then the school psychologist will assume the role of evaluator. The school psychologist will collect any information necessary to determine eligibility for special education services. This will involve cognitive, adaptive and achievement testing, and interviews with the parents.

If autism or AS is suspected, completing the autism-related checklist, such as the Childhood Autism Rating Scale (Schopler, et al., 1988) or the Gilliam Autism Rating Scale (Gilliam, 1995), or some of the newer rating scales for individuals with AS is necessary. The evaluation team or the school psychologist usually completes this form. However, if the school district has no personnel with autism expertise, they may contract with local or state professionals (such as a child psychiatrist or neurologist) to make the determination.

Once all of the information is assembled, the parents will be called in to review the results. If the student is being diagnosed with PDD, autism, AS, or other disability, the parents will be provided with information regarding the diagnosis, and encouraged to seek information outside of the school (though many schools won't pay for further testing). They then proceed to an Individual Education Plan (IEP) meeting.

An IEP is a legal document that will drive the child's education program through the school year. Parents will participate in a new IEP at least once a year, but several meetings are possible, depending on the situation. However, one IEP meeting is usually enough for most people to endure! When schools and parents do not agree on what should be in the IEP, then subsequent meetings will have to be held to work out the differences. Differences, which cannot be worked out in school-level meetings, will proceed to the next step of mediation. Here, a neutral mediator listens to both sides and makes a decision.

Again, if the parents or school disagree with the mediator, then the next step is due process, involving a judge. Theoretically, a dispute between home and school can go all the way to the Supreme Court, as some do, though this takes years and involves numerous lawyers before reaching a final decision. Sometimes the student is beyond school-age when the final results are in, so it is imperative that both school and home learn to work together to solve the differences so that the student will not suffer when opinions clash.

A. Issues to Consider for a Middle School IEP

An IEP will provide your student with the exact program for her educational years. The brief number of issues mentioned here are not meant to fully inform the parent or school of all the issues they will need to address with their particular student.

As a middle school student, however, there are some basic components of the IEP that need to be considered during these years that might not have been in the elementary years. They include:

- Objectives to cover budding sexuality issues: Students enter puberty in these years, and most students with autism do not understand the changes that are occurring in their bodies. Many embarrassing situations can be presented by students placing their hands inside their pants, not attending to grooming skills well enough, making embarrassing comments to others, etc.

- Organizational skills: Students with autism are required to conduct much of their day independently, especially in the use of their organizational skills. Homework assignments need to be remembered, the agenda book filled in, and work submitted.

- Long term goals: Transition planning should not be relegated to the high school years alone. This is a hard topic for parents, but must be started at this age.

- Full social skills assessment as well as pragmatic language assessment.

- Full-profile of functioning: Remember the graph on page 11 - not just the high levels, but also which areas need remediation. Recognition of the true profile.

- Occupational therapy (yes, it may still be needed!).

- Peer programming

- Support levels from paraprofessionals.

- Alternatives to work output (computer generated work, note takers, oral tests, etc.)

Some of these topics are self-explanatory, but others will be detailed below.

B. Necessary Supports

Middle school students with autism/AS who are in inclusive settings usually require various level of support to succeed. This is often in the form of paraprofessional support. This will vary from one student to the next, of course, but it is clearly needed with students with autism. To be placed in this environment without the supports necessary can be devastating to both the student with the disability and to her typical classmates.

Sufficient support is often the one component that will determine success or failure. Although many of our students with autism or AS can function academically at a high level, they often suffer socially because the support systems are not in place. Therefore it is crucial that this element be closely scrutinized to determine what is necessary and what areas the student can be relied upon to perform independently.

Decisions surrounding support levels have a number of issues that must be considered:

<u>What is the level of maladaptive behaviors with this student?</u> How often will the paraprofessional have to intercede? How frequent are the intervals for reinforcement on the behavior plan? How obtrusive will the reinforcement be to the general education classroom?

<u>What is the level of communication with this student?</u> Is he using a picture board? A PECS (Bondy) system? Voice-output device? Can the paraprofessional operate the system adequately? Can the student use the system independently, and if so, under what conditions?

<u>How much modification of academics is needed?</u> What can be done by the paraprofessional, and what must be done by the teacher? Is the student using a modified curriculum or an alternative curriculum? Portions of an alternative curriculum can be difficult to administer in a general education classroom. What can be, and what can't be?

<u>How much data collection is needed for this student?</u> Is this system extensive, or can it be done quite easily in a general education classroom? What forms are used with this student? How much must be done by the teacher, and how much can be done by support personnel?

<u>What self-help skills are of concern for this student?</u> Will they need someone to assist them with the toilet? Washing hands? What about eating, or even carrying the tray in the cafeteria? What about maneuvering around the school? Can they find their way independently or will they need help?

<u>How does this student interact socially with others?</u> Is he isolative? Does he walk down the hallway without speaking to anyone? Does he need cues to seek proximity, to initiate or respond to others?

<u>What is the level of fine motor skills?</u> Is writing difficult for this student? What can he do by himself and where does he need help? Are there occupational therapy goals that must be worked on in the general education setting? Is he using a word processor to do the written performance part of school work?

<u>What is the level of motivation for this student?</u> Does the paraprofessional need to use on-going creative ideas to maintain motivation for task completion? Will the behavior program suffice for the entire day, week or month, or does it need daily adjustment by an adult who can "think on her feet?"

A transition portfolio form is found in the Appendix of this book. It may help in identifying the student's strengths and areas of challenge, to lessen any problems for the student moving into or out of middle school, or to another grade within middle school. Check it out!

These, as well as thousands of other questions that parents or teachers may ask, can be the basis of determining levels of support personnel at the IEP meeting. However, once levels of support staff are determined, you can't stop there. Before the program can be implemented, there are additional issues to discuss at this meeting.

C. Questions to Ask About Paraprofessionals or Teacher's Assistants

<u>How will this person be trained?</u> Too often, we ask a tremendous amount of work from the paraprofessional without providing her with the training necessary to do her job. Who will train this person? Will she be given articles to read? Attend a workshop? Learn on-the-job? Have a mentor? Are there county-level requirements for paraprofessionals in the school system?

Often, parapros must earn a number of credits within the year to gain or renew certification. What are your county's requirements? Will this person be trained to increase the level of the student's independent functioning, or is it likely that the student will become cue-dependent upon her? Does she understand that she is to work hard to eliminate her own job with the student? Will regular evaluations be conducted on this person? What recourse does the teacher or parent have if it just isn't working out?

<u>What is this person's experience with autism?</u> Is this a veteran paraprofessional? Whom has she worked with prior to this student? Just because she has had experience with

students with autism does not mean, automatically, that she will bond with this new student, or know instinctively what to do with them in adverse situations. Students with autism vary greatly; this paraprofessional will need to understand the new student's profile and ability levels.

Who will supervise this paraprofessional? Being a paraprofessional with a student in middle school regular education classrooms often means that she is on her own, with little or no supervision. Many times, regular education teachers don't feel it is their responsibility to supervise a special education staff member, nor do they want to take on this added level of duties. So the decision needs to be made about how levels of supervision will be conducted and by what teaching staff.

Will the paraprofessional staff member be pulled away from the student to perform other school duties? School principals like to pull paraprofessionals to conduct other school duties, such as helping with bus duties, giving out medications, helping to set up the cafeteria for special events, copying papers for teachers, etc. This list goes on and on. Will this happen with the support person for this student?

Is this person solely dedicated to this student, or will she be shared with another student? If shared, how much time will be spent away from this student? Will it be possible to change her assigned times as the student changes behaviors?

What levels of positive redirections are usually delivered by this paraprofessional? (This is assuming that the paraprofessional has already been chosen.) Is this a naturally supportive person? Does she use more positive cues than negative cues? What is her personality like? (Most parents will not be given a chance to participate in the selection process of a paraprofessional, but if they can find out any of these answers, it will be somewhat easier to predict how they will do with this student.)

Who takes over when the paraprofessional eats lunch or is on break? When is her lunch break scheduled? If she takes lunch at the same time as the student, she will not be available to conduct small group social skills activities during the lunch time. If not her, then who? Will the student be able to be independent at the time the paraprofessional goes on lunch break? What's the best time to schedule it?

Both parents and teachers will want each of these questions answered. Most, but not always all, can be answered at the IEP.

Paraprofessionals are usually extremely dedicated individuals. Don't form opinions without documentation. Paraprofessionals can make or break a program. It is certainly worth the time and effort to view these questions up front, provide the training, offer ongoing supervision and plenty of reinforcement from both parents and teachers.

A good, solid paraprofessional is worth her weight in gold. These hard-working folks deserve much credit, but rarely get it. School systems aren't set up to conduct as much reinforcement as these people earn. Parents should jump into the breach and offer on-going support for what they do with our students in the way of notes to the principal, special awards at banquets, invitations to go to local conferences, or even just a pan of brownies. Reinforce, reinforce, reinforce. They need as much reinforcement as our students, for they work just as hard!

5

Behavior Programming in Middle School

Before we begin, we must make it *crystal clear* that there are varying levels of maladaptive behavior that students with autism may exhibit. Most teachers' levels of expertise in behavior programming are sufficient to deal with the average range of behaviors seen in students with autism (though this author does realize that there are varying opinions on this matter). Those of us who work with students with this disorder, however, sometimes see students with extremely high levels of self-injurious or aggressive behaviors which prove resistant to the "run-of-the-mill" behavior programming that is conducted in a classroom. Indeed, individuals with this disorder may exhibit very severe behaviors, behaviors that are not easily extinguished by a special or regular education teacher who has read basic steps in a textbook (this book included).

By middle school, some students with autism can display resistive behaviors that many teachers have probably attempted to eliminate over the years through various inconsistently applied behavior plans. Some resistant behaviors, such as self-injurious behaviors or more outwardly aggressive behaviors toward others, will probably not prove responsive to the level of behavior programming that the usual teacher training has afforded them.

Specifically trained behavior analysts who have worked with students or clients with this kind of behavior MUST address these severe behaviors. Some children even require clinical functional analysis of behavior in order to solve the mystery of function and the events driving the behavior. Special education teachers, and indeed, many school behavior specialists, have not received the level of training that is needed to conduct clinical functional analysis or extremely intensive behavior programs. This is not meant to be an insult to teachers or their training. Severe behaviors require extensive and systematic application of clinical-level behavior programming and ongoing analysis designed to detect minute changes in behavior.

Teachers who have a student with this level of behavior will usually recognize the need for extensive help in addressing these behaviors! Any behavior that is long-standing, causes injury, interferes with programming for weeks on end, or has driven parents to seek out-of-home placement, is a behavior that should send the teacher scrambling for the special education director and for support services from qualified behavior specialists or analysts.

Unfortunately, these talented individuals are hard to find. Special education directors should look to universities, hospitals or private practices to find a clinical psychologist adept in systematic behavior analysis and programming. It goes without saying that these behaviors are best addressed in the early years to prevent the situation from growing worse as the student ages, requiring even more intensive intervention or hospitalization. If the student has this level of aberrant behavior, options should be explored immediately.

Suspension is not a solution to these behaviors! Suspending the student for exhibiting these behaviors only delays solving the problem. Suspension also allows further time to entrench the behavior, which usually makes the situation worse and also loses valuable instruction time. Suspension also sets the child up for learning the wrong lessons about such behaviors. Schools' "zero tolerance" policies often mean that our students with autism are suspended from school because they exhibit a behavior that breaks the rules established by the local school board. We all know and understand why these rules were established, but unfortunately students with autism/AS are often the recipients of the fall-out on this style of discipline policy. They exhibit behaviors directly linked to their impairment in communication and social skills, leading to confusion for both the administration and the student.

Parents look to those who teach students who exhibit significant behaviors such as self-injury or severe aggression as people who can help solve this problem. Don't let them down and ignore the situation, please. Find the specialists who can help. No child should have to grow up in restraints (or be led off in handcuffs by the police) because no one wants to face the issue.

Having said all that, we must remember that there are still many, many behaviors that students with autism exhibit on a daily basis that can be affected by a teacher's level of behavior programming. So please, teachers, do not lose heart! Remember that there are many levels of autism, and many levels of inappropriate behaviors. Positive behavior programming is much more about structure, consistency and follow-through by the teacher than it is about behaviors.

Nevertheless, behavior programming in middle school can still be more difficult than it was in elementary school. Consistency in implementation is one of the largest problems when considering inclusive settings at this age because more teachers are involved with the student in middle school than in elementary school. Collaboration between the special education teacher and several regular education teachers poses many logistical problems. All behavioral programming, whether for extinguishing minor inappropriate behaviors or addressing more significant behaviors, demands that all teachers involved operate with the same information on addressing these behaviors. Teachers may handle a behavior differently than the paraprofessional, causing the student to become confused and upset.

By middle school, students with autism can have well-cemented behaviors, ones they have exhibited for many years. In this instance, it will be neither easy nor quick to replace them with appropriate behaviors.

If the middle school special education teacher wishes to conduct inclusion programming with her students, she will have to address social behaviors in light of both typical students and of teacher expectations. She will need to prepare her students for expected behaviors in the hallways and classrooms, as well as for frequent transitions throughout the day. The student must be prepared to deal with noisy cafeterias, clanging lockers, and sensitive (and sometimes manipulative) peers. Behaviors that may have passed as acceptable or tolerable in a self-contained classroom, where no one else could see them, will not stand the light of day in a more natural setting. As a result, much planning and analysis must be conducted even before beginning this process of including students with autism, much less have it be successful. After all, anyone can throw a student into regular education and have the student fail. It takes insight, practice and commitment to make it a success.

<u>Let's start at the beginning.</u> There are many steps to addressing behavior programming for a middle-school age student with autism. The following steps may prove helpful when developing behavior programs for your students. They are not meant to be all encompassing. Teachers can find many other textbooks that outline behavior programs using different scenarios, steps, and key words. However, the goal will always be the same: that the student exhibit increasing amounts of appropriate behaviors in natural settings. This text will outline positive behavior plans, as opposed to negative or aversive behavior plans.

At this point, we will assume that you have a student who exhibits inappropriate behaviors. You know that these behaviors will set him apart from his typical peers in an inclusive setting, and you wish to alleviate that situation. Where do you start?

A. Behavior Analysis

Step One: BEGIN WITH YOURSELF

Do not begin with the student! Teachers and parents quickly assume that the student or child is totally at fault and immediately start analyzing the child. But when a full analysis is conducted, it often reveals that teachers and support staff treat behaviors differently, so everyone is analyzing different behaviors instead of their own teaching styles.

This is a huge mistake! Teachers or parents often make statements such as "The student will not do what I ask him to do," or, "He is being manipulative and ignoring me," or "He will do it for _____ (the parent or teacher) and not me! Why?"

So, begin with yourself.

Teachers' styles of delivering instructions may not be clear enough for the student to understand and comply, or the teacher may give conflicting instructions. Also, the parents handle the same scenario much differently than the teacher. Moms and dads can vary in how they deliver instructions or requests, leaving the child very confused. To help make sure that everyone is approaching the problem behavior from the same point of view, the following questions should be asked prior to behavior analysis:

1. Are my instructions clear?
2. Am I using too many words in sentences?
3. Am I consistent with the student's other teachers who handle this situation?
4. Do I deliver the same consequences or reinforcements as other staff members?
5. Am I using back-up visual materials with my instructions?
6. Do I allow enough time for processing?
7. Am I asking for too much information from the student?
8. Are my expectations too high (or low) for this student?

Teachers and parents can think of thousands of questions to ask themselves regarding consistency of instruction. Without addressing these and similar questions first, it is unfair to set up a behavior program for a student when the core features of the overall problem behavior lie with the teaching staff (at home or at school).

Step Two: CONSIDER MEDICAL REASONS FOR THE BEHAVIOR

Remember, students with autism/AS are often unable to communicate that they are in pain or are feeling ill. They may also have adverse reactions to pain caused by illness or injury. Therefore, when there is a rapid change in behavior, teachers and parents should consider medical reasons for the change. Students exhibiting severe regression in appropriate behaviors may have an ear infection, sore throat, headache, pin worms, bowel obstruction, or other medical problems. Take temperatures; observe facial coloring; look for nasal discharges; check with parents about vomiting or diarrhea; ask numerous questions of yourself, other teaching staff, and parents in the hopes of identifying any underlying medical problems that may contribute to a change in behavior.

Step Three: ENVIRONMENTAL REASONS FOR THE BEHAVIOR

Look to the environment next to identify possible reasons for inappropriate behaviors. Students with autism often demonstrate difficulties with sensory input, becoming overly sensitive to noises, smells, large spaces, unfamiliar people, etc. Examine the classrooms and other settings for areas of difficulty for your student. Middle schools are much noisier than elementary schools, and students are assaulted with a variety of noises that they didn't contend with in the elementary schools. Is he upset because there is chaos in the room? Are there too many transitions in the schedule? Are the loud noises from the air conditioning unit down the hall bothersome, or is he fearful of the noises generated by the toilets flushing in the bathroom across the hall?

Once identified, desensitization procedures can help the student begin to overcome fear of the noise or other stimulus. Perhaps changes in daily schedules can help in eliminating the problem behavior by reducing tension over transitions, thereby escaping the situation that causes anxiety.

Students with autism are greatly affected by sensory issues and/or environmental conditions in middle school. Sensory issues must be analyzed and considered, especially for the student with Asperger's Syndrome. It is sometimes very easy to change a maladaptive behavior for an adaptive behavior by simply changing the environment.

But, there is a real caution here! Having an inclusive philosophy means that we are teaching students to live in the natural environment. We cannot accomplish this by changing the entire environment so it no longer resembles the natural environment. Looking to the environment for areas to change is fine in the natural order of analysis of behavior. We must make sure, however, that we do not change the environment too much, preventing the student from generalizing the skills learned. We cannot change the environment to resemble a self-contained classroom or we will be right back where we started, with the student shut away from the world.

So analyze wisely. Change what you must, then teach and help the student to adapt, understand, tolerate, and escape when they must, or accept situations that they will be expected to live with as an adult. Gradual introduction of environmental factors can help students learn to trust and adapt without causing undue stress. There will, of course, be some environmental conditions that can never be tolerated no matter what the preparation, but this will vary from individual to individual.

Step Four: INDENTIFYING THE TARGETED BEHAVIOR

What behaviors are considered inappropriate at this age? Acceptable middle school behaviors differ from those of elementary school because the typical students are less accepting than elementary school students and because the student is now physically much larger and stronger. In kindergarten, wandering around the classroom during instruction time was tolerated, but it is not acceptable in middle school. In elementary school talking out of turn can be overlooked in the general chaos that reigns, but middle school teachers will not accept it.

Teachers should identify what behaviors are unacceptable in the various environments throughout the day. Voice modulation is not as big a deal in P.E. as it is in language arts. On-task engagement may not be as crucial during music as it is in math. Decisions will have to be made regarding which behaviors, in particular, are considered by all staff members to be targeted for change. This is not an individual teacher decision! It must be a team approach if there is any hope of changing this behavior in a middle school setting.

Once the targeted behaviors are identified, they need to be defined. Targeted behaviors are never behaviors that teachers "think" may occur but must be seen to be identified. Individual teachers and parents usually have their own point of view of a behavior. Team members need to come to a consensus as to what behavior the student is exhibiting to which everyone objects. Is he hitting using his left hand? Does he spit first? Is he running in circles before falling to the floor? Is he using verbal aggression? Do you recognize the behaviors from a video the student has seen? Is it a single behavior or a combination of behaviors? If only one component of a multi-component behavior is addressed, it could make the situation worse. Therefore, make sure all of the staff understands the exact behavior that is being targeted. Examples of defined behaviors are as follows:

> **Talking out of turn:** During class discussions, Jennifer calls out answers to questions posed to the classroom without raising her hand. She will begin to bounce up and down in her seat and call out the answer without waiting to be asked. Also, she uses an overly loud voice when calling out answers.
>
> **Out of seat and wandering behavior:** During group discussions, Sean leaves his seat and his task to wander over to the window. While at the window, he does not respond to cues to return to his seat, but instead picks up the window plants to examine the leaves and dirt.
>
> **Yelling and/or cursing/crying:** Given instructions to read a passage in language arts class, Kevin begins to yell at the teaching staff using curse words or loud vocalizations and continues for approximately five minutes. He sometimes also cries when yelling. He will eventually comply with directions after the peers are made to stop talking to him and looking at him.

Aggression and vocalizations: Hitting, kicking, or pushing another individual. When upset (not yet determined why), Tommy approaches another individual (usually, but not only, the teacher) and uses his right hand to hit her on the arm. Tommy usually hits two to three times (on average) in rapid succession while yelling and screaming. Rarely, he will also kick.

Rocking behavior: At times during core academics, though fully engaged with his work, Todd exhibits a full-body rocking behavior in his seat. His chair is often rocked onto the back legs, causing it, on occasion, to fall backwards onto the floor. He will then get up, look around the room at the students and then sit back down.

As shown in the examples, all teachers must be <u>very clear</u> as to how the inappropriate behavior looks, so that others can readily recognize it when the student exhibits it. There should be no question of, "did it occur or not?" In this way, all should easily recognize the targeted behavior when seen each and every time. If the behavior can't be recognized, then re-definitions should be considered, or the IEP manager should order a review of the present definitions.

Step Five: DATA COLLECTION

Data collection is a crucial step in changing behaviors.

When asked immediately after an inappropriate behavior how long it lasted, a parent or teacher will tell you that the behavior went on "forever!" However, it rarely does. While the instinctive reaction is that the behavior continued for a long time, the reality recorded objectively by the observer was that the behavior was short-lived. A systematic recording of facts must replace perceived observations as a foundation for decision making.

First, data collection will provide insight into the targeted behavior, informed decisions can be made regarding intervention strategies, and assumptions based on reactions to the behavior can be avoided. Reacting instinctively to an inappropriate behavior to eliminate harm to the student or others may be all right in the heat of the moment. But reactive decisions should never be the basis of a solid behavior program. After all, instinctive reactions are not the best way to handle a behavior since instincts vary dramatically between people.

Although teachers do not like to hear the words "collect data on this," it must be done. It is not a step that can be eliminated in the rush to solve the problem. Even in an excellent behavior program that has been up and running for some time, simple data collection can verify that the targeted behavior has been reduced or extinguished, thereby eliminating the need for the plan altogether. Baseline data can show you how severe the behavior is. If it rarely occurs, then is it really a behavior problem? In some cases, yes; in others, no.

Collecting data can be conducted by the parents as well, and is very useful in providing information across all settings. Don't miss this step! Information gained from data collection can tell you, among others:

1. How often the behavior occurs in a day/week/month?
2. Who is usually involved with the behavior?
3. How long does it last (no, it is NOT forever)?
4. What activities are usually involved?
5. What time of day is the behavior more prevalent?

Those collecting data on a targeted behavior can use the following form quite easily. A full-sized form can be found in the Appendix at the back of this textbook.

DATA COLLECTION FORM

Student: _____ DOB: _____

Week of: _____ Teacher: _____

Targeted behavior(s):_____

Date/Time	Setting/Activity People Involved	Antecedent/ Triggering event	Description of Behavior	Duration/How long did it last?	Consequence/ Others' response	Comments

Each time the targeted behavior occurs, the teaching staff or the parents should fill out the form, explaining what happened. Definitions for each include:

Date/Time: (Self-explanatory)

Setting: Classroom, hallway, gym, cafeteria, etc.
Activity: What activity was occurring (Language Arts, P.E. math, etc.)
People involved: Who was interacting with the student when the behavior occurred, or immediately before it?

Antecedent: (Triggering event). What occurred just before the behavior made the student react? Antecedents are sometimes very difficult to discern; however, try to record everything that happened just before the behavior occurred. Look for facts, not suppositions.

Description of Behavior: Describe fully the behavior exhibited, especially any variations from the defined targeted behavior.

Consequence: What were the consequences of the behavior? What did the student gain, lose, avoid or have reinforced by exhibiting the behavior? Did the student go to time-out? Was he escorted out of the room? Lose privileges? Helped to calm down and return to task? Escape the task entirely? What actions did staff take towards the student as a result of the behavior?

Write down as much information as you can immediately, or as soon as possible after the behavior. Waiting until the end of the day usually means loss of valuable memories of the event, leading to wrong conclusions and incorrect behavior programming. Therefore, data should be collected as quickly as possible after the event. The teacher or paraprofessional can record this information as long as it gets on paper as quickly as possible.

The above form is excellent for describing behaviors and taking data on a daily basis. However, this information must be processed and analyzed over time by qualified staff members who are well-versed in behavior programming. The form can be used for multiple targeted behaviors, but you will also need to see frequency over time on each behavior in order to decide if the behavior is increasing or decreasing.

The following form is an example of using the computer to conduct simple tabulations of behaviors.

Student Name: _____DOB:_____
Targeted Behavior: _____
Chart dates: From:_____To:_____

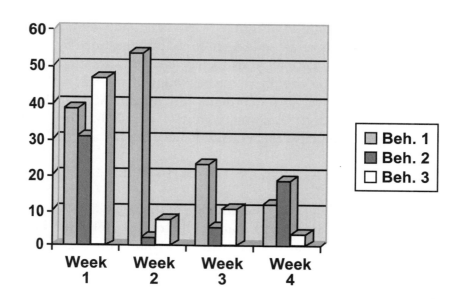

Or, it could be as simple as the following form:

Targeted behavior:_____

Graph Dates From:_____ To:_____

10	10	10	10	10	10	10
9	9	9	9	9	9	9
8	8	8	8	8	8	8
7	7	7	7	7	7	7
6	6	6	6	6	6	6
5	5	5	5	5	5	5
4	4	4	4	4	4	4
3	3	3	3	3	3	3
2	2	2	2	2	2	2
1	1	1	1	1	1	1

Date: _____

By circling or slashing the number of times the behavior occurred in each day (or each week for longer time spans), simple graphs can be drawn to show how the behavior changes over time. This is a simple method to view frequency over time, and does not take extensive expertise.

Data collection and graphs provide great insight into subtle patterns that may have developed over time, and can be helpful in pinpointing increases or decreases in behavior occurrence. Data can offer the strongest support for teaching styles and activities, behavior plans and transition plans. Without it, teachers not only eliminate a great teaching tool, they also lay themselves wide open for harsh questions by supervisors, parents, and unfortunately in today's litigious society, lawyers and judges, as to why data was not collected. Data collection should be the backbone of any teacher's program for students with any disability, as well as for students with autism/AS in inclusive settings. This disability is confusing enough. Don't place yourself at risk for more confusion by eliminating the one major supportive tool educators have readily at hand.

Step Six: DETERMINE THE FUNCTION OF THE BEHAVIOR

Analyze the data collected to determine the function of the behavior. Why did the student use this particular behavior at this time? What was he trying to tell you? What was behind the behavior being exhibited? Behaviors rarely happen "out of the blue." They almost always have a purpose behind them. "Behavior" is often tied to one of four things (though there can many others, these should be considered and explored first; look beyond them in research journals, if necessary):

1. To make a demand
2. To state a refusal
3. To escape something
4. For self-gratification

Analysis of behavior can be quite complex, requiring different viewpoints and analysis of the data collected, simply because students with autism often exhibit very confusing behaviors. Therefore it is often valuable to have someone specializing in behavior modification strategies analyze the data to help make decisions for behavior programming. Once the function of the behavior is determined, it does not mean it is the end of the behavior analysis. The above steps are only part of the scope of changing a student's behavior. Now, where do you go from here?

B. Positive Behavior Systems

You have now analyzed yourself, the staff, changed what was necessary in the environment, defined the behavior, collected data and determined the function of that behavior. Now, what do you do? How do you get the student to eliminate or decrease this inappropriate behavior? Again, let's take this step by step.

Step One: IDENTIFY THE REPLACEMENT BEHAVIOR

If you don't like what the student is doing (the maladaptive behavior) what do you want him to do instead? Keep this in mind always! You can't just demand that the student stop what he is doing. For him, the behavior is working to gain what he wants and it doesn't matter to him that it is not working for you. It serves his purpose, and if you want him to change the behavior, you must find a replacement behavior that serves that same purpose. Suppressing the behavior may result in a larger, more severe behavior in its place. You will need to teach him the replacement behavior. After all, if it were in his repertoire already, he would have been using it instead of the inappropriate behavior.

Finding a replacement behavior usually leads directly back to the student's communication system. By middle school, many students with autism have been through every available communication system, never settling on one method. Analyze his present system. Chances are it is not adequate or you wouldn't have inappropriate behaviors. Ask the speech therapist to provide you with updated information on speech evaluation. Evaluate not only where his receptive and expressive skills lay, but also analyze exactly what the student must do to communicate his wants and needs. What action does the student choose when he wants a drink of water, needs help, or wants to use the bathroom? What does he do if he just wants to say "No," or "Yes?" These are questions that must be answered if you want to provide the student with alternatives to maladaptive behaviors. Several forms are available from various professionals in the field (Donnellan; Prizant, etc.) that can help you analyze communication systems and determine replacements for inappropriate behaviors. These forms are quite easy to use and they provide extensive information on the methods the student uses to communicate his wants and needs. Ask your school to locate one for you to use on your student - you will find references in the Appendix of this book.

Step Two: MOTIVATION SYSTEMS

Even though you teach a new behavior you will need to provide reinforcement. Do not expect the student to be inwardly driven to perform this new behavior just because you asked her to. She may not have a clue as to why you want this new behavior rather than the old one! Providing reinforcement for exhibiting the new behavior adds motivation and acceptance for the student. Sometimes, this means just a social reinforcement such as a smile, a pat on the back, or telling her that what she did was great, etc. Other times, it may mean providing the student with a primary (edibles) or secondary (tokens) reinforcer. You must pair something enjoyable with the new behavior to make it more attractive for the student to use and remember. If you gave the student something he doesn't like, odds are he is not going to want to exhibit the new behavior. Therefore, you should conduct a motivational survey to determine what motivates this student.

A motivational survey is outlined in the Appendix of this book. Both school and home should conduct this survey to gain a better insight into what reinforces the student across all settings.

When looking toward reinforcers, do not be confined to just what is found in a classroom. Look beyond the classroom into the greater environment, such as the school or community. Homes and schools can collaborate on reinforcement systems, allow the student to earn points at school, and gain reinforcement at home. However, many students with autism/AS can't wait long for a reinforcer, and a more immediate system should be in place. Waiting for the end of the day may be too long for some. Many students with autism enjoy computers, art, reading or drawing, and other academic subjects that can be adapted to include a reinforcing effect for the student's program. Be creative and flexible when choosing motivators! Don't forget the social component. Just because our students have difficulty with social skills does not mean that they are uninterested in social interactions. Some students with autism love to be the center of attention and will do anything to gain it from others. Use this to teach new skills. Believe it or not, this is a positive!

Step Three: DIFFERENTIAL REINFORCEMENT SYSTEMS (DRO)

DRO programs are some of the most effective behavioral systems used by teachers to affect behavior. Differential programs reinforce a student for exhibiting the more desirable, appropriate behavior during intervals throughout the targeted time. You can reinforce the student for <u>omitting</u> a behavior during a time frame (DRO), or exhibiting an <u>"other"</u> behavior (also a "DRO" program). You can reinforce for exhibiting a behavior that is <u>incompatible</u> (DRI), an <u>alternative</u> behavior (DRA), or for exhibiting the same inappropriate behavior fewer and fewer times (DRL – <u>lower</u> rates of behavior).

Whichever program you choose, consistency in programming will be the key to success. Let's start with examples of each of the programs listed above, to make sure that you have gained an understanding of each.

Targeted Behavior: Screaming

<u>DRO</u> - (Omission): Reinforce a student every _____ minutes for not screaming.
<u>DRO</u> - (Other): Reinforce a student during an interval for stating "I'm angry!"
<u>DRI</u> - (Incompatible behavior): Reinforce the student for "zipping lips" and being quiet on an interval system. (Can't scream and zip lips at the same time.)
<u>DRA</u> -(Alternate behavior): Reinforce the student for running a lap in the gym to wear off angry feelings.
<u>DRL</u> - (Lower rates of behavior): Reinforce the student for screaming fewer times during one day than the previous day.

Differential systems can help to turn many maladaptive behaviors into more positive, acceptable behaviors. There are a few "musts" with differential systems, however. They are:

1. The program must be explained in concrete form to the student so that she will understand better. Eliminate abstract concepts on any form used.
2. Target the visual depiction to the age of the student. Don't use "kid-cute" systems for budding teenagers in middle school if they are designed for elementary school. Do not use systems that will call undue attention to the student, making them appear even more different from the typical student than they already are.
3. For students with autism, whether in regular education or special education, visual depictions will most likely be necessary to ensure understanding. If the student does not understand the system, do not count on it being effective.
4. Teachers must be trained in the system so that all use it consistently.
5. Motivators need to be built into the system so that the student fully understands what she will gain by working so hard on appropriate behaviors.

6. Systems need to cross all environments pertaining to the behavior. Some can be site-specific, but if a behavior shows up in one environment, it will almost certainly show up in others. Make sure that the system can be used wherever the behavior occurs.

7. MOTIVATORS CHANGE! Don't rely on the student being motivated forever by the same object or activity. Their opinions change as to what is fun or exciting and they may want to earn something different the next time. Keep ahead of the student by conducting motivational surveys so that you have a list of objects and strategies to choose from.

8. Once behaviors are under control, put them on maintenance and choose others that need targeting.

9. Wean the student off the systems as needed, but be ready to re-institute them if necessary. Don't wean too quickly: ensure appropriate behaviors have been placed in long-term memory.

Step Four: OPPORTUNITIES TO EXHIBIT THE NEW BEHAVIOR

Completing the behavior modification cycle means to orchestrate opportunities to practice the new, replacement behavior. It is not likely that, after teaching and reinforcing a new behavior when needed, the next opportunity where the behavior is called for results in the student exhibiting this new behavior. If it were that easy for students with autism to learn a new behavior, teachers or parents would have corrected all their maladaptive behaviors years ago. Remember "regression to the mean" or average. Your intent must be to have the student practice the new behavior so many times that their average behavior is raised to the point that they exhibit fewer inappropriate behaviors than appropriate behaviors.

Simply put, if you want their average behavior to be better, you must provide them with numerous opportunities to practice the behaviors you expect of them for their behavior to move along an upward path. This can mean dozens or even hundreds of chances a day to practice the new behavior so that they can become used to performing it. You will have to actually orchestrate these opportunities, rather than just waiting for opportunities to present themselves. After much practice, when the time comes and it is crucial that they exhibit the new behavior instead of the old, their average behavior will have risen enough for them to demonstrate a better, more appropriate behavior without even thinking about it.

C. Reactive/Crisis Plans

Set Up Your Crisis or Reactive Plan

When an undesirable behavior is occurring enough for teachers and parents to be worried, a reactive plan must be considered to protect not only the student with autism, but the teachers and other students as well. This student is now larger and more powerful. Exact responses need to be clearly stated. How do you want staff to handle the student when it does occur? Define EXACTLY what the staff member accompanying the student at that moment will do when the behavior is exhibited. To protect the student, staff and other students, precise directions must be spelled out for all to understand and use when needed. Sometimes staff will need to practice how they will use the reactive plans to make sure that they are performing them correctly. Consistency is very important in reactive plans.

Crisis plans usually teach more about how to *prevent* the situation than how to "handle" it. By going through this process, much will be made clear to the staff.

While reactive plans are certainly necessary, problems arise when the teacher has only reactive plans without positive behavior plans. That scenario can be disastrous! Don't leave the student confused about what will happen when a behavior is exhibited. Rather, carry out the consequences as calmly as you can, with as few negative connotations as possible and get the student back on track quickly. Don't cause the student anxiety by constantly reminding them about the consequences if they misbehave. Remember that behavioral consequences will handle the situation at that moment and put out that fire, but rarely do anything to teach new replacement skills over time. Look to a positive behavior program to accomplish that task.

Finally, students need to know how their behavior affects others. In today's society, when the student reaches adulthood, there will be very real consequences for inappropriate behaviors in public. While the student is still in school, especially middle school, we have golden opportunities to teach reasonable consequences without crushing the student emotionally.

Some school districts use formal programs which teach crisis management procedures. They also have standardized forms for student management, using gentle tactics that do not harm students or staff. These programs require sessions from trained personnel and continuous practice to remain proficient.

Teachers seldom get enough practice in these techniques to stay familiar with them, and consequently have weak skills when they're most needed. Unless schools schedule routine reviews and practices for the teachers, schools may waste money and resources. Recently, Smith-Myles (2001) stated that she wishes all teachers would stay current on the proper methods of restraining students. This is mostly because the instructions gained in these lectures are on prevention and how to control a student without hurting him. If you have a student with overly aggressive behaviors, the management method should be the least restrictive possible, and applied in such a manner that it solves the situation instead of creating a bigger one. Also remember - restraining techniques usually escalate inappropriate behaviors with students with autism/AS. So try to avoid these at all costs!

Although reactive plans are important to ensure consistency among staff treating the behaviors, teachers should not fall into the trap of believing those plans are enough. Reactive plans, alone, do NOT teach behaviors for students with autism. They appear to work very well with typical students, as you can assume that the student will know what he did wrong and understand that he should not do it again. You CANNOT, however, assume this with autistic students. Students with autism/AS view the world differently than typical individuals and behave differently as a result. Therefore, you must teach them the new replacement behaviors because they do not understand the appropriate behaviors to use to achieve the same result. Reactive plans just put out fires each time the behavior is exhibited. In order to help the student find a new way to behave, you must actually teach the replacement skill.

When devising reactive plans, make sure you understand that the real emphasis of behavior programming is on the <u>prevention and analysis</u> of the behaviors. Stay ahead of the behavior problem, instead of playing catch-up and implementing only the reactive program. Also, ensure both teachers and paraprofessionals are thoroughly trained and regularly refreshed in applying crisis management skills to behavior modification. This simple step will help ensure that injuries are prevented and both students and teachers are protected.

Behavior Management of Middle School Students with Asperger's Syndrome

Students with AS often pose difficult and puzzling problems when faced with the demands of the typical middle school academics and environments. Although we have spent time talking about "autism/AS," students with Asperger's Syndrome have unique qualities that often allow for more inclusive programming. They also require teachers to consider behavior programs to shape the student's actions and reactions to conform to middle school expectations in the generalized setting.

However, if the student with AS is in regular education classes, he may not appreciate behavior programs which set him apart from the other students or which call undue attention to his problems. In addition, if the student is provided with paraprofessional support while in the general education environment, he may actually become angry and belligerent when the support staff attempts to modify his behavior because the student is aware that the other students are watching.

Students with AS often just want to fit in with their peers, and do not want anything done, including behavior management, which will make them look different from their classmates. This puts pressure on the teachers to find creative methods to change behavior in the classroom. Special education teachers should look to the regular education teacher and the methods used with the typical students when setting up supplemental behavior programs for those with AS. She can then add additional, possibly even surreptitious methods to implement the program without adding stress for the student.

Special education teachers can use the same behavior plan in the classroom, but will likely have to add positive systems of motivation. For example, if the regular teacher hands out certificates of merit and demerit for credit or misbehavior, then the special education teacher can add motivational systems for the AS student on top of the already existing system. Another example: she can offer the student incentives for earning a set number of merit certificates during each period to be cashed in, either in the special education room or with a particular mentor teacher.

Decompression Time: Students with AS also benefit from time to decompress from the overly-stimulating environment of regular education. Students with this disorder often try very hard to fit into the regular classroom. This creates stress and continuous pressure for the child. Delays or differences in processing, fine or gross motor delays, poor written performance, loud noises, low grades or the inability to finish all work in the length of time allotted can lead to low self-worth and increased stress levels. If these stresses cause behavioral outbursts, self-regulation programs can be taught to the student to recognize when he is exhibiting high-levels of anxiety, or is under undue pressure.

Let's look at one simple plan:

> *"David" is allowed a certain number of credits (a number set jointly by both the teacher and "David") to use throughout his day. He may cash them in with whatever teacher he is with and "escape" the classroom to go to a "safe room" or home base for a grace period (10 minutes maximum) to re-group and calm down. The number of credits can be determined by the student's level of anxiety, academic struggles and coping skills.*

Other methods may need to be found to assist a student with AS to regulate behavior, such as behavioral contracting, teacher verification systems of behavior, point systems, earning unusual motivators who which tap into perseverative interests, etc.

A final note on behavior programming. This student is now in middle school and it won't be long before he is in high school and beyond. If he has gotten into middle school and still has many aberrant behaviors, *now is the time to eliminate those behaviors!* You don't have a moment to waste. These students have much to learn before leaving the educational system and aberrant behaviors will only hinder their growth. So please, do not put off addressing long-standing behaviors any more. Begin immediately so the student will have the best chance of learning and growing for the future.

6

Academic Issues for Middle School Students

Middle school academics are a new and different experience for your child with autism or Asperger's Syndrome. Parents face a big shock from the loss of the well loved, nurturing elementary school teachers who were able to coax reluctant students into performing. But middle school can be an exciting time, as well. The following topics regarding middle school academics are offered as areas to consider as you go about making decisions for including your child or student. Remember – designing a perfect program for a student is very dependent upon having full knowledge of the options - all of them.

A. Middle School Academic Environment

While middle school academics are unlike the elementary grade levels, many middle school and special education teachers want inclusion programs for their students. Because of academic concerns, these teachers will need well-honed public relations skills to get past the resistance of some of the regular education teachers. Please don't hold this against them—in their roles as teachers, they are expected and pressured to have all of their students reach academic standards set by the school district and/or state. This presents incredible stress for new, inexperienced, or even veteran teachers. Also, in many schools throughout the nation, regular education teachers are not used to students with severe cognitive or behavioral disabilities in their classrooms, unless they teach in an enlightened school district.

Middle school teachers are a special breed and are often faced with students in their most chaotic time of life. They must meet the challenges of adolescence head-on, break up destructive cliques, help shy students fit in, or ride herd on misplaced exuberance. They must also respond to the demands of their school district. Dealing with these issues can result in tension for students as well as for special education teachers. Conversely, a team of inclusion-experienced middle school teachers can take all of the nervousness and tension out of the situation and make for an enjoyable program.

There is no rule as to where on the autism spectrum resistance to inclusion will occur. However, if the student with autism can handle the regular education academic demands, it is likely that he or she will be viewed, initially, as a candidate for the general education classrooms. (I know IDEA states that it should work the other way around, but we are talking reality here.) Although behaviors end up taking precedence over academic abilities when considering inclusive students, many teachers are frightened over the big "A" word (autism or Asperger's) and may pose resistance to inclusion even before they meet the student. This may be against the law, but it happens.

When approaching middle school teachers, the parent or IEP team must first educate the new teachers on the incoming student's strengths, and areas of need last. These teachers need to be able to understand the "student first, disability last" way of thinking. All students will benefit by having their teachers view them as individuals who happen to have differences, rather than as disruptive or inappropriate students.

Middle schools are run differently in different states, but on the whole, subjects are usually divided into four main areas: language arts, science, math and social studies. In addition to these four classes, your student will usually have a chance to choose two exploratory classes per grading period. Sometimes, middle school grade levels are divided into certain groups, such as "communities," and rotate through the exploratories together, so that your student will rotate with the same students. One large disadvantage for our students in middle school is that, in rotating, teachers are not as coordinated on programs as we need them to be. Often, the math teacher never talks to the science teacher, or the language arts teacher never sees the exploratory teachers regarding a student, other than at individual education program (IEP) meetings. This is an area that needs to be discussed at the IEP and measures taken which will lead to close coordination. (See Treatment Team Meetings in Chapter 8).

Exploratories can, but do not always, include the following: P.E., technology, band, art, computer science, foreign language, chorus, home economics, certain musical instruments, drama, health, etc. *(Exploratory means that the student can select among elective courses, which change at the end of each grading segment.)* With an IEP, your student will get the chance to choose which exploratory they would like to have and which ones they want to eliminate. Sometimes exploratories can be repeated, if necessary.

To learn more about your student's potential academic schedule options, call your district middle school and obtain the necessary information to help you make plans for your child's future in middle school and see what course work is available for selection. This can help you start to gain an idea of the class schedules that your student will follow.

B. Functional Curriculum versus Academic Curriculum

When a student is placed in an inclusive environment, especially in middle school, teachers and parents alike often ask: "What about a curriculum for those students with severe cognitive impairment? Is it no longer needed?" "When will they learn to be independent in their adaptive skills?" Clearly, this is a decision that must be made by the IEP team for each student with autism, but the team must realize that there are some issues that must be thoroughly discussed prior to making final decisions. Brown, et al. (1991), states

> *The effects of severe intellectual disabilities cannot be denied, ignored, or minimized in importance. They must be acknowledged and accounted for in educational services.*

This section will attempt to provide insight into the sticky subject of functional skills versus inclusive programming so the IEP team can assess the topic thoroughly prior to making decisions.

In elementary school functional curricula take the form of toilet training, independent eating, dressing, and of course, basic academic skills. Students learn activities such as holding a pencil correctly, writing on the lines, identifying colors receptively and expressively, and other skills that will help the student progress, learn and maneuver around the school sufficiently. In middle school we hope most of these objectives have already been met. So why do we need to consider functional skills at this age?

We already know that, when working in the field of autism, many students experience cognitive delays or impairments, which makes it difficult for them to fully grasp and master higher-level academics. But should we absolutely give up trying to teach them this knowledge? Many students with autism can contribute and participate in higher-level academics through modifications and accommodations to the core curriculum. Students with disabilities, even students with severe profiles, can participate to their individual potential in general education classes when they have the proper supports and assistance from trained personnel. However, even with proper supports, the fact remains that it is easier to accomplish this mission of inclusionary education for academics and functional skills in elementary school than it is in middle school because academics and adaptive skills for the typical students increase rapidly. Should we continue, then, to try inclusion if some of our students can't keep up? Or should we teach only a functional curriculum?

I said this earlier, but I think it bears repeating:

We know students with autism have uneven skill development, and they need strategies that require task analysis, repetition of instruction, and demonstration from positive models. Teaching in the natural environment allows for better understanding of needed skills, and the "natural environment" for a school-age child is the wider school system-the inclusion classroom.

We conduct inclusive programs to gain the strong social and language skills, but what about other life skills beyond social skills and language, such as community skills, self-help or independent living skills?

Teachers do families no favors when they graduate students who are able to work with other people, but who still lack job skills or independent adaptive skills. Adults with this disability will have many demands placed on them from the community. The skills and knowledge necessary to meet these demands must be taught in the natural environment. These are not learned magically after they graduate from middle or high school.

We have many adults with this disorder sitting in their homes with no skills to access the community environments, and who require daily assistance to conduct even the most basic adaptive skills. At this age, the term "inclusion" must take on a much wider goal than just the school. This is far different from what we experienced in the elementary years. Broaden your scope and your definition of this term of "inclusion" in middle school to include the community setting. It is not necessary to include the entire community until high school, but learned skills should begin to spread beyond the school doors at this time.

Therefore, parents have some very serious topics to discuss while soliciting opinions from their child's teachers. In an ideal world, all students would be educated in the regular education classes. But do all parents want that for their children? And is it the best source of education for all students? Middle schools offer many opportunities for inclusive experiences for their child with autism. They should also offer opportunities for community-based instruction in the areas of shopping, restaurant dining, cooking, recreational/leisure experiences and other skills listed under "functional academic" or "functional curriculum." These skills will increase quality of life for both the student and the family, and should be considered by the IEP team in light of the particular student.

I do not intend to make this important decision of functional versus academic content for parents or teachers, nor do I suggest that access to typical students be eliminated in favor of the functional curriculum. Rather, I intend to pose questions for the parents and IEP team members to help determine the outcomes possible for your child. Obviously, the resulting program will look different for a student with autism who has higher abilities than it will for someone with severe challenges.

Programs will also look different for a student with mild Asperger's Syndrome than it will for someone who has a much more severe AS profile. Therefore, the following issues are offered in hopes that they will help make your decision on how to approach functional versus core academics.

Parents' long-term goals

This is a hard topic for parents. Usually, parents of students with autism/AS are more concerned with getting through each day than worrying about 20 years down the road.

However, it is important to start thinking about this issue when your student is in middle school. By this time, you will have a better idea of the functioning levels of your child in all areas, and what strategies are necessary to teach them simple and complex routines. Think about:

❑ Will they go on to college or take post-secondary classes? Where?
❑ Where do you see them living as a student – at home, in a dorm or apartment, supported living, etc?
❑ Do you think they will keep their apartment clean without you there? (By the way, many typical young adults don't do this!)
❑ How much independence do you think they will achieve?
❑ Will they have a job, ride the bus, deposit their own paycheck and balance their bank statement?
❑ Will they have a driver's license?
❑ Will they be able to read a recipe, gather the ingredients and use the stove?
❑ What about shopping and going to restaurants, to the local pool or movie theater?

These are only a few of the very tough issues to think about. But begin at this time in your child's life to make decisions as to how many of the functional objectives must be imbedded into an inclusion program.

Teacher's Analysis of the Student

Teachers also need to assess the student's transition into middle school to help the parents make this difficult decision. Although it will not be the teacher's decision as to what this student will be doing as an adult, it will be her expertise that will determine if he makes his goals. Teachers have students for a short time before adulthood – they will be gone in the blink of an eye. Therefore, it is essential that you participate in the analysis process that will determine how much of the functional curriculum will need to be included in this student's inclusion program. As adults, *it is absolutely essential* that they be as independent as possible. Society's support systems often diminish or disappear due to tax and budget cuts or family crisis. We never do our students a favor by graduating them to sit at home for the rest of their lives because of a lack of foresight on our part. So to help in this process, ask yourself the following questions regarding your student:

❑ Forget test results – where does your student function adaptively?
❑ How long does it take your student to learn a simple routine?
❑ How many steps are in this student's analysis for self-care?
❑ How independent are they for communicating wants & needs?
❑ Are all their self-help skills independent?
❑ What are their decision-making processes like?

❑ Can they achieve high levels of independence in a variety of domains?

❑ How can you imbed functional skills into an inclusion program?

There are probably thousands of questions that can be posed for making decisions on functional living skills. There are also excellent curricula that can help you make decisions regarding this important area. Wise teachers and parents should investigate as many as possible to find the one that will prove the most helpful. A full adaptive behavior assessment should be conducted on any middle school child with an autism spectrum disorder (and even one with Asperger's Syndrome). One to investigate might be *Checklist of Adaptive Living Skills* (CALS) by Morreau & Bruininks, (1991). The *Vineland Adaptive Behavior Scales* (Sparrow, et. al., 1984) can also provide insight into this area and allow for suggestions for IEP objectives.

Begin the assessment process during the last year of elementary school, prior to the last IEP, so the team will have sufficient information to render appropriate decisions regarding functional versus academic curriculum.

Another Note Regarding Students With Asperger's Syndrome:

Just because your student or child has Asperger's Syndrome and a higher level of cognitive functioning, do not assume that their adaptive living skills are age-typical. Many students with AS demonstrate low adaptive behaviors, such as appropriate grooming or bathroom skills (wiping themselves independently or washing their hands afterwards, flushing the toilet after use) which will pose uncomfortable situations around middle school peers. Because of this lack of appropriate adaptive skills, peers may not view this student as a candidate for friendships because he poses embarrassing situations. Students with AS are notoriously oblivious to dress styles, hairstyles, etc., and are immature when making decisions regarding their everyday adaptive behaviors in light of the social norms. Therefore, it is *extremely important* to conduct adaptive living skills on late elementary students with AS, viewing them through the lens of middle school peers, so that issues which will isolate them from peers can be identified and addressed early on. Look beyond adaptive living skills to adaptive social skills as well.

View this student objectively to help them assimilate into middle school. Include other topics such as:

- manner of gait (middle schoolers notice coordination and manner of walking, unfortunately!),

- music selection (is your child with AS into the latest music trends?),

- favorite television programs (students with AS often have an immature selection of favorites on TV, such as cartoons or elementary versions of shows),

- magazines they like to read (comic books versus teen pop magazines), etc.

They may be able to perform academically, but many students with AS face isolation and depression due to lack of ability to fit in with their peers. Adaptive and daily functional skills have a whole new meaning for students with AS!

C. Academic Modifications

Inclusion students with either autism or AS will likely need to have some form of academic modification while in their inclusion classes. Students with AS may not be seen as needing the modifications that some students with autism do, but in reality, they may require more! Students with AS likely need curriculum modifications due to deficits in fine motor control. This makes written expressions and grasping abstract concepts difficult. They may also need a lighter workload in some subjects to prevent loss of motivation. Students with autism, because of the high prevalence of cognitive impairment, will usually require modification to the content being delivered. Regardless of the spectrum of disorder or cognitive functioning, teachers and parents should consider all of the following areas that may need modification to make it easier for the inclusion student to follow the core curriculum and/or remain in the regular education classroom. See Appendix for some titles suggested by Deschene, C., Ebeling, D. G., Sprague, J. (1994).

Subjects

❏ Some subjects will be more difficult for our students than others. One student may have strengths in math, while others may not. Some courses may be required, while some are electives. Pick and choose appropriate classes, eliminating the courses with which you know your student will have problems. For example, although most subjects are required, some are electives that can sometimes be eliminated if they prove to be too difficult. This is also the time of your child's life when you can explore other subjects that may fascinate them and allow them to learn new methods or outlets for expression. A student with a gift for foreign languages may use an exploratory in Spanish or French to open the door for extended studies in high school. So do not dismiss subject materials out of hand. They may prove to be the saving factor for your child's education.

❏ Examine how abstract the subject material will be. Is there a lot of problem solving involved? How can the subject be made more concrete? Can the student have pre-teaching sessions on class content prior to the day it is taught? Pre-teaching often works much better than post-teaching.

Timing

❑ Middle school academics have deadlines imposed by teachers and the state. Tests are timed and come at predictable points in the year. Students with autism-related disorders often run afoul of the timeliness aspect of middle school academics. Pressure to perform is a factor that, for our student is often impossible to meet. Therefore, start considering how the timing aspect of the academic load can be lessened to prevent problems.

❑ Take standardized tests over a period of days, administering small portions on subsequent days.

❑ Set timers to help the student realize passage of time. One excellent timer on the market is *Time Timer* (Generaction, Inc.) which, instead of an audible ring, has a visual cue to show passage of time. This can help a student stay on task and understand the time limitations of tests. Others may also be on the market – look in special education school catalogs for a variety.

Level of difficulty

❑ Break the tasks into smaller steps, helping the student realize that smaller components of the material can decrease difficulty.

❑ Pre-teach subject material and eliminate or explain abstract components.

❑ Provide supplemental materials to help explain the main topics, characters or themes of the material presented.

❑ Use graphic organizers and mapping to help the student understand the relationships between components, making it seem much less difficult.

Environmental conditions

❑ Many students with this disorder are uncomfortable in certain settings, such as sitting too close to peers or near chaotic traffic patterns. Assess the setting where the student is working. They could possibly be moved to a quieter or calmer place in the classroom, away from distractions, but still near other students.

Work load

❑ Students with autism or AS often cannot keep up with the heavy demands of middle school academics. Conversely, some of our students may require specific-subject enrichment classes because they are far ahead of their peers. Students with autism/ AS may demonstrate either profile, surprisingly. Therefore, middle school teachers must analyze their student to determine a sufficient workload to allow understanding and challenge, without overloading or underloading the student.

❑ Amount of homework also needs close examination. Students with AS are often considered to be able to handle more than they actually can because their cognitive ability would denote it. Unfortunately, the large amount of homework is usually a strong factor in turning our students with AS off of school, leading many to drop out at this age. Teachers must be very careful not to expect more than the student with AS is capable of.

Receptive ability levels

❑ Cognitive receptive ability levels will determine how much instruction the student can understand, or the lengths to which one must go to attain higher levels of understanding. A majority of students with autism will have some form of cognitive impairment, leading to confusion if the material is targeted too high for them. Middle school teachers will need to take their lead from the special education teacher as to where to target materials for receptive understanding. Other methods that can help understanding include visual back-up systems, charts, task lists, tape recorded materials, maps, graphs or outlines. Supplemental textbooks (see resource list) can help the student better understand the content by posing it in a different light.

Expressive ability levels

❑ Individuals with these disorders have varying degrees of difficulty in expressing themselves because of difficulty with expressive language. Teachers should seek other modes to relate information, such as writing out their answers to questions, drawing the answers, choosing the answers from a selection, using the computer keyboard or word processor, or pointing/gesturing to the correct answer. Don't assume that just because a student isn't expressive that he cannot communicate his wishes or needs. Ask the speech therapist to find other methods for the student to express answers.

❑ Typical middle school students will not generally be used to having someone in the classroom who does not participate orally. At the beginning of school, they may require some explanation as to the methods needed to help this student fully engage in the class, so that they can help him or her become a true member of the class. Peers are often much better at teaching academics to students with disabilities, due to their age-level creativity and enthusiasm. Please try to enlist them in your efforts to assimilate this student, and look into the peer programming portion of this book for ideas in this area.

Levels of staffing

❑ As stated previously, students with autism/AS who are in middle school sometimes require a paraprofessional to assist them with their academic production. However, this is a tricky business in middle school for some of our students, especially students with AS. Students who have classic autism are often viewed as being in need of assistance, thereby justifying paraprofessional support. However, although they may require assistance, students with AS usually do not appear different than other students, and the student usually wants to keep it that way! The presence of the aide calls unwanted attention to the student, and causes the peers to make erroneous assumptions, or to distance themselves, thereby eliminating possible friendships. Teachers must consider ways of providing the student with the support needed without "hovering" over them. An excellent model for offering covert assistance is the co- taught or "collaborative" class (having both special and regular education teachers in the room) which can offer all students help, both special and regular education, without seeming to belong to "just one student." Many middle schools offer co-taught classes to help support their students with disabilities, thereby impacting students with autism/AS.

❑ For students with autism with more severe profiles of this disorder, levels of support may also vary. Focus should be on how to deliver instruction without causing the student to become cue-dependent. Walking around the classroom can give the student the cues needed without standing or sitting continually next to the student. Using visual systems to prompt the student to continue with his work, even without a direct prompt from the paraprofessional or aide, can keep them on-task without direct assistance.

❑ Much analysis and thought should precede decisions about levels of support for a student in middle school. The ultimate goal is independence, or at least dependence on natural cues, rather than on a support person. Paraprofessionals usually try to do their job too well – thereby crowding the student and providing more prompts than necessary. Their job should be to put themselves out of work by having the student become independent. Many paraprofessionals will find this paradoxical and will not understand how to achieve it. Therefore, the task falls to the special education teacher to appropriately train her paraprofessionals in methods of student support.

Partial Participation

❑ Students with autism may not be able to fully participate in the core academics at this level of education. However, more is learned in a classroom than just academics. Appropriate physical proximity, interaction skills, conversational skills, understanding non-verbal body language, and recognizing natural cues to work quietly are all skills learned in class. Middle school classrooms house a wealth of non-academic information that can help all students be better prepared for adult life.

❑ Students with autism should participate in the academic content to the fullest measure of their ability. There are many items and materials beyond these pages that should be investigated. Some offer step-by-step instructions for dissecting material to make it applicable for your student. Use the resource list at the end of this book for suggestions on these excellent materials for adapting instruction.

D. Diplomas — What Colleges Want

Although this is only middle school, it is not too early to think about what type of diploma your student or child will receive when they graduate from high school. Some schools, counties, or states may require that the student choose his type of high school diploma (college prep; college prep with distinction; tech prep; vocational; special education, etc.) in eighth grade. Diplomas are (and should be) tough to earn. Freshman year involves taking courses that assign certain credits toward that diploma. Therefore, the eighth grader may have to decide at this time what diploma to aim for so that coursework can be arranged for the freshman year.

It is not too early to begin educating yourself on options. It would be helpful to learn what requirements are necessary for admittance into colleges, universities, tech schools or vocational schools, or community colleges since they vary tremendously and you have time. Requirements for admittance into a computer or engineering college vary from one college to another, as does admittance for history, math, auto mechanics, fashion, etc.

Many students with autism can easily acquire a regular education diploma, and some can not. However, those who can't make the traditional trek may not be able to do so for a variety of reasons, other than their cognitive functioning ability levels. Students with autism who can often absorb or comprehend the material cannot always handle the overall environment of middle school. They may be incapable of sitting and listening to lectures for 55 to 90 minutes (traditional versus block scheduling, respectively), answering questions within time limits, or producing written material. Because of their disability and the difficulties they have encountered in school, many of our students are under special education and have an IEP. This frequently means that they are preparing for a special education certification.

This may be a large mistake for some students.

Many students with autism or AS who have such a tough time in middle or high school may blossom in college. Individuals who demonstrate unusual behaviors and mannerisms looked on as "weird" in grade school may discover that those behaviors fit right into the free lifestyle of college students. After all, college students are often referred to as "weird," or "those college kids" by parents.

It is not unusual to find half of the college campus sitting in front of a computer for three days straight, without eating or socializing, while writing reports, theses or dissertations. Clothes may go weeks without washing, balanced diets go out the window and students start friendships with others who share interests and behaviors. (This author is speaking from experience, sad to say!). Many of our students with autism who demonstrate idiosyncratic behaviors fit right in with other students who demonstrate similar idiosyncratic behaviors but have not been declared "autistic."

Unfortunately many of our students with this particular profile (many with AS) opt out of a regular education diploma track to go on and earn a special education certificate. As a result they do not pass the necessary tests to gain a regular education diploma. Also, since they have opted out of the crucial classes, they do not have the necessary information to acquire a GED. Again, unfortunately (and this is indeed unfortunate), with a special education certificate, and without passing the exit exams or gaining a GED, they will not likely get into **any** college, even if they want to take just one class – such as a computer class. This is a rude awakening to many families. Many believed that if they could just hold it together through the lower grades, their child's genius would be recognized in college, he'd specialize in paleontology, fractals, machine learning, statistical methods or other highly specialized fields, and everything would turn out for the best. With a special education certificate alone, this is not likely unless they go back to high school and take the courses and tests that they skipped.

Don't forget about SAT's, either. Even though some of our students graduate with a high school diploma and pass all the exit exams, they may not get into the college of their choice because their SAT scores are not high enough for the one area they are trying to get into. One institution of higher learning has a minimum of 325 on the test for admittance; another 1350 (1600 is a perfect score). Taking the test multiple times (start with the PSAT and then the SAT) can help to raise the scores.

If your student will not be going on to the university level, certain requirements can keep them out of the best vocational or technical schools. Find out who requires SATs, ACTs, graduation exit exams, GED's, particular courses for a particular subject, apprenticeships, references, experience, etc.

If your student is programmed for a regular education diploma and things start to fall apart in high school, it may or may not be easy to shift to a special education certificate to relieve the pressure.

It is much harder to do the opposite, though—to shift over to a regular education diploma when the student has been in special education for some time. If you plan to switch, your child may have many classes to make up. It depends on how long they were in that program and which courses they elected out of. They may even have to attend additional years in high school, but remember, in special education, they can go until they turn 21.

It is also sometimes easy to shift from a regular education diploma to a vocational diploma, but not so easy to do the reverse. This is why parents may have to assess their child's options early to make preliminary decisions regarding which diploma should be earned. It is best to leave as many options open as possible when lining up classes for the ninth grade year. Fully explore academic modifications (mentioned in the previous chapter) to see how your child can fit into the regular education arena, or how the child can be in special education and take as many of the classes as necessary for a regular education diploma.

Although it is preferable that students with autism or AS who are able to go on to higher education should have a regular education diploma, do not assume that we should denigrate a special education certificate. A special education certificate was never meant to have the negative connotations that it has acquired over the years. A special education certificate should mean that this student had an incredibly rich experience in the areas that are needed, lining this student up for very specialized work and living opportunities and solid adaptive skills. This student has had, after all, the benefit of highly specialized teachers and loving parents doing nothing but examining his program time and time again. They analyzed, problem-solved, streamlined, formulated, and manipulated, and otherwise designed the program so this student would go on to enjoy a full life. The typical student rarely has the advantage of so many people helping him design his education. The question remains as to why our students, who obviously have had so many advantages, are still not able to capitalize on these advantages? Universities and colleges should be beating our doors down trying to gain these students for their programs, not turning them away. Also, why are so many of our students not able to gain and keep a job after graduation?

The sad fact is that a special education certificate has come to mean many things and is not viewed favorably by agencies that require regular education diplomas. However, when asked recently (phone survey by this author), dozens of colleges and universities stated that they would accept a special education certificate as long as the student has passed a GED (without it, no admittance). Allowances were not made for a student who was auditing classes or just registering as a non-degree student and taking one or two classes. Many students with autism who have specific areas of interest would benefit tremendously by taking one or two specialized classes. This would help them to find a job in their area, yet they are potentially eliminated because they can't sit and take a GED test.

We can get around this problem by careful examination of the student beginning in middle school, by examining potential classes, by making realistic projections for their future, by modifying classes wherever we need to, and by challenging the boundaries of autism and cognitive deficits. Isn't this the true definition of school?

Examples of Requirements: (varies by state)

Parents and teachers should examine-

❑ Regular Ed Diplomas:
    ❑ College Prep with Distinction
    ❑ College Prep
    ❑ Technical Prep with Distinction
    ❑ Technical Prep

❑ Vocational Diploma

❑ Special Education Diploma

❑ Certificate of Attendance

E. Foreign Language Requirement

Middle school offers the first real opportunity to experience a foreign language. The hope is that the students will become interested in the language and the culture and will want to pursue it further in high school. Some of our elementary students are exposed to languages in elementary school, but middle school offers more intensive study within the exploratory series. (Exploratory series means that the student can select amongst elective courses, which will change at the end of each grading segment.)

Many students with autism or AS struggle with the foreign language requirement because of the memorization and analysis of what appear to be non-words and meanings. Most students with this disability have great difficulty with information processing with the English language (or their own native language) without trying to assimilate another language. However, there is a select group of students with this disorder who absolutely blossom when taking a foreign language. They seem to have a natural talent for learning the complicated conjugations of words and alternate meanings of phrases. Students have been found to do very well with Spanish, French, and even German. Therefore, do not dismiss out of hand the foreign language component from your child or student's syllabus. They may very well prove to you and to past teachers that they can learn this subject material very well.

It is usually wise to explore the foreign language requirement in middle school if possible, since colleges will require a foreign language class in high school. Taking a foreign language exploratory in middle school will give your student a leg up on the more intensive, high school language class. It can, at the very least, show your student which language NOT to take in high school.

Once your student has determined which foreign language to take, parents can help their child understand or master this subject:

❑ Supply other materials not provided by the school. School stores in your community usually have workbooks, stories, or tapes in foreign languages to help reinforce the process.

❑ Find materials home-schooled children use. There are many companies that offer materials in foreign languages to supplement the school program.

❑ Introduce your child to someone who is fluent in the language who may act as a tutor.

❑ Card games and board games are helpful. Play them often and make sure that they are FUN games, not just educational ones, if you want them to continue to be interested in the language.

❑ Find comic books in the foreign language. Middle school students LOVE comic books, especially weird and unusual ones. Just get someone to proof the content before giving it to your child to make sure it maintains your personal, parental standards. But a note of caution – don't make the comic books too "politically correct" or you will lose the interest of the middle schooler. At this age, they need to believe that they are "getting away with something right under the parent's eye" – providing more incentive to learn to read the materials!

Even with all of this effort your child may struggle with the foreign language requirement in a particular area. This may exempt them from admittance into a college later on; do not give up hope. Have the student try other languages at home to see if he can more easily understand the material in this new language. Students with autism or AS often surprise us (actually, they do so continually)! Just because they bomb out on one language doesn't mean that they will in other languages. Your child or student is in middle school. So be patient.

If this child still struggles in high school to complete the foreign language requirement, it may be necessary to find out what can be substituted for the foreign language requirement and if it can be waived for a regular education diploma. Accommodations may be made to modify the requirements for a diploma since there is a formal diagnosis, but this varies in each state.

Let's Talk Reality About Parental Expectations

A note about planning for your child's post-secondary future – it is wise, helpful, encouraging and loving to have the highest expectations for your child and want them to experience college as so many typical students do. But remember many typical students don't go to college and are successful anyway. When planning for students with special needs to enjoy the adult life common to typical students, we must recognize that many of our students will also not go on to post-secondary education. There is nothing wrong with this! The hopes and dreams are great for this child, but be realistic as you encourage and explore options throughout middle school. Know when to pull back and when not to pressure them. Too much pressure, too much stress, and they are soon turned off school and drop out. You'd be surprised how many of our students with autism/AS actually do drop out of school during the middle school years, and never walk through the door of a school again. So while you are planning to complete tough courses like foreign language, be careful not to overstress your child with pressure to perform. There is a careful balance between challenging the student and orchestrating too much pressure and it will be different from student to student.

F. Block Scheduling

Among educators and parents, block scheduling is very controversial. Research can be found to support both the "pros" and "cons" of this style of teaching. Judgements will not be made here as to which is better for students with autism/AS, since our students vary in their responses to it. Block scheduling began in the secondary schools, though it has now moved into the middle schools. Parents should explore this subject thoroughly if their child will attend a school that uses this style of teaching.

Block scheduling and traditional scheduling in middle school each offer opportunities and drawbacks for students with autism and AS alike.

Examples of Block Scheduling:

Monday	Tuesday	Wednesday	Thursday	Friday
A (70 min seg)	A (70 min)	A (2.5 hours)	B (2.5 hours)	A (70 min)
B	B	—	—	B
Lunch	Lunch	Lunch	Lunch	Lunch
C	C	C (2.5 hours)	D (2.5 hours)	C
D	D	—	—	D

Monday	Tuesday	Wednesday	Thursday	Friday
1	2	1	2	1
3	Enrichment	3	Enrichment	3
Lunch	Lunch	Lunch	Lunch	Lunch
5	4	5	4	5
7	6	7	6	7

Monday	Tuesday	Wednesday	Thursday	Friday
1	2	1	2	1 2
3	Lecture	3	Lecture	3 Homeroom
5	6	5	6	5 6
7	8	7	8	7

Traditional scheduling means that the student has every subject chosen for that quarter (or semester) every day, based upon a 50 minute schedule. The student has, at the most, 10 minutes to transition to the next class. Fifty-minute classes usually offer enough time for the typical students to perform all that is necessary for the coursework. It may not be enough time for autistic/AS students, though. In traditional scheduling, if the student is having difficulty with a particular subject, teacher, or peer, he will have to endure it every day. It may be hard for them to control behaviors under these conditions.

Block scheduling "is the breaking up of school time into blocks or units of classroom time with periods that are either twice as long or four times as long" as traditional scheduling (www.netaxs.com). It is different from traditional scheduling in that the student still has the same number of classes, but does not meet with them every day. They can have alternating schedules, sometimes referred to as "A" days and "B" days.

Individual classes last 90 minutes in one variety of block scheduling. The student still meets with all of their classes during the week. The student has more time to process and problem solve the materials, to further explore concepts, to have better opportunities to discuss material amongst themselves, to participate in group activities, and to generally obtain a more in-depth experience with each class. The hope is that, over the course of the quarter or semester, students will actually learn more about each particular subject, rather than rushing through everything in 55 minutes, stretching and dissecting the material over the course of a five-day-a-week class schedule (4 X 4 plan).

There are many types of schedules possible in block scheduling. As you can see from the examples above, there are generally four large segments each day, each representing a different class or subject. The segments are divided up on some days, and left as is on others. Length of each block is usually 90 minutes, but they can stretch to two segments or more. The student takes this arrangement of classes until the end of the grading period, then switches classes. Schools and counties decide which pattern they want to use for their participating schools.

After viewing the schedules, you can quickly understand why students with autism or AS sometimes have difficulty with this style of programming. Although the number of transitions each day may be less than a traditional schedule, each day is different, greatly taxing organizational skills. If the student is sick one day or out with a doctor's appointment, he will have to rely quite heavily on his schedule list to find where he should be for the next day. Also, if he misses a class, it is the equivalent of two classes on a traditional schedule. This can be disconcerting and provoke anxiety for the student with autism or AS.

Is this a better method for teaching all students? Is it a better method for teaching students with autism/AS? Research appears to be divided on this subject. Although block scheduling is used more in high school, middle schools are using it more as well. The benefits to students with autism/AS vary as much as the disability does. For students who have intense interests in one subject, this form of scheduling can work out nicely. Students have extra time in one day to learn in greater detail and to explore relevant areas than they would under a more traditional schedule. For classes that are not especially liked, however, this can be torture. Sitting for a long time in one room with the same teacher can also be quite trying for our students. They can possibly begin to exhibit behaviors arising from their frustration. Also, group activities are often conducted more in block scheduling than traditional scheduling since the class has more time. Group activities, in which each student is expected to contribute and participate, can be hard for students with autism/AS, leading to frustration and possible behaviors.

If your student will be attending a middle school that has implemented block scheduling, begin now to obtain information regarding options, pattern of scheduling, etc. Request *detailed information* about the program that the school will be using and conduct your own research on that particular style. These schedules can easily be found on the Internet. Multiple references can be found to increase your knowledge regarding this subject. Also, find out which middle school has a traditional schedule in case your student works and studies better under that style of programming. In that case you may wish to request a transfer.

G. Teacher Expectations

Middle school teacher expectations and opinions can be quite different from elementary school, and they vary widely at this age. Middle school teachers understand that they must prepare their students for the high-pressure world of high school society, as well as get them academically ready for the more adult world of high school. This is manifested in many ways, but it usually means that teachers expect their students to be more independent than they were in elementary school. The wise teacher will understand that her sixth grade students do not walk through the door on day one, organized and independent of a teacher's nurturing talents.

Some wonderful middle school teachers understand that they need to actually _teach_ organizational skills, not just expect them to be exhibited all at once. Although you would assume that all sixth grade teachers realize this, many require the student to have mastered organizational skills the first day of school. It is best for you to talk to each teacher your student will have and try to determine their expectations. You may also need to inform them that organizational skills are one area in which students with this disability struggle.

Students with autism/AS usually require intense instruction in organization of materials, time, assignments, homework and other areas of middle school learning. Verbal instruction in these areas will not likely be enough; students usually require visual cues and direct prompts, which are sometimes based upon a behavioral performance chart, to help them learn how to become independent. The following organizational skills should be assessed in late elementary school, to ensure readiness for middle school:

1. Arriving promptly at school.
2. Getting correct books out at appropriate times.
3. Having necessary materials (pen, paper, sharpened pencil).
4. Turning in assignments on time.
5. Prompt and appropriate use of agenda books to write down assignments.
6. Taking home the necessary materials for homework.
7. Collecting appropriate materials for upcoming assignments.
8. Putting personal items in the locker at the correct time.
9. Gathering up all of their personal possessions at the end of each class.
10. Using the bathroom between classes instead of having to leave class.
11. Projecting needs for the next class.
12. Having a neat desk during class.
13. Using the proper notebook for the proper class.
14. Appropriate use of study time.

There are most likely many other areas that require organizational instruction, but this list will help you do a preliminary assessment of your elementary student so that he will be better able to meet teacher expectations. Make sure that organizational skills are covered in your child's IEP so that teachers will fully understand the ramifications of this. If this student with autism/AS requires modification in this area, middle school teachers must fully understand that they must do the modification – it is not an option, but a <u>necessity</u> required by law (IEP).

Middle school teachers also expect that assignments are done (full assignments) and that they are turned in on time. Many teachers will be flexible with the student who has an identified disability and an IEP. The problems arise when the student truly has this particular disability and is not yet diagnosed, such as a student with Asperger's Syndrome. Teachers can become very angry if they perceive that the student is being disrespectful by not turning in work, turning in incomplete assignments, or generally disobeying teacher's instructions. Along with being angry with the student, teachers can quickly form long-lasting negative opinions and become even more rigid in their expectations of the student.

Sometimes, parents may not wish to disclose the disability to their child's teachers. In this author's opinion, this situation sets the student up for failure. The student will be severely punished for having an undisclosed disability.

Teachers need to know and understand about autism or Asperger's Syndrome before negative opinions form that may harm your child. Teachers will then have the opportunity to research the subject and to coordinate efforts with other teachers who can assist with the student's program throughout middle school. They can also modify academics, workloads, assignments, and other general expectations if they understand the disability. But without this knowledge, students with AS are often under tremendous pressure to "shape up" and "perform like the other students," which is impossible for them.

This knowledge will not solve all the problems of teacher expectations, though. Much will depend on what the teachers <u>do</u> with this information and how they shape their opinions based upon this new-found knowledge. If they still do not wish to accept the disability or do not agree to change their expectations, then they may broadcast their displeasure about the student to others.

Passing along information and opinions to others not involved means that the grapevine is alive and well in your school. The news will almost certainly get to the typical students, eventually causing embarrassment or distress to the student with the disability (who may or may not even know that he has a disability). Great care must be taken to keep this information confidential. Although parents are often reluctant to suggest that teachers violate confidentiality rules, this subject MUST be discussed at the IEP because mistakes happen, rumors are started, and papers are left sitting on desks where they can be viewed by others.

Taking precautions to safeguard information and opinions makes for a better environment for the student and peers alike. Typical middle school students can be tough on students with autism/AS. Training select peers (with parent permission) by providing information and a chance to ask questions is better for the students than having peers gain information through uncontrolled circumstances.

Teacher expectations are ultimately driven by their own experiences, by state and county guidelines, and by prior knowledge of the student. Make sure that the middle school teachers have the information they need to make appropriate decisions about your child. A sample transition portfolio is in the Appendix to help with the decision process, and many issues can be solved through discussions in the IEP. However, if parents encounter resistance and unacceptable solutions to the problems of academic expectations, parents should request that these teachers receive training in the legalities of an IEP, and possibly seek the help of an advocate. We hope, however, that this step will not be needed, as that can have the ramifications of building walls between home and school.

H. Academic Intensity

The intensity of academics in middle school can be quite surprising, though sixth grade teachers will usually begin the year with review material and increase the demands gradually over the course of the year. The review material will be the foundation upon which the student will learn new concepts, so it is important to maintain attention and focus on this issue. Parents should make sure that their child understands the review material and content during this time. They can do this through evening reviews, supplemental materials and possible tutoring, either during school or outside school time – even during summer, if necessary. It is important for your child to stay academically at grade level, if at all possible, in order to eliminate or reduce the need for academic modifications.

Most parents understand that middle school academics are more intensive than elementary school, but few parents realize just how much more intense it really becomes. Middle schools will usually tell parents to expect their child to have homework two or three nights a week. However, that is usually an underestimation. It is not unusual to have homework each and every night, for 1-3 hours, especially as the student ages through middle school.

Long projects must be completed over a given time, meaning the student must work on portions of it for days on end. Tests also take on added importance, since this is an indicator of what track they will be on for high school. Many parents, when first introduced to their child's middle school, become disheartened when hearing all that their little boy or girl needs to accomplish. They may also be shocked about the environment of middle school – the fact that there can be 2000 students, gigantic cafeterias and gymnasiums, and seemingly thousands of teachers to educate this one person. The task of getting their child through middle school seems daunting to both parents and teachers of students with autism/AS.

This is the time for everyone to take a deep breath. Let's just take the academic intensity for now and forget, for the moment, the other 1,999 students and the cafeteria noise. Parents will want to know from the child's IEP team:

❑ What concepts are being taught at this level, or grade, or class?

❑ How abstract will the material become?

❑ How much of the workload is fact-based, and how much of the work demands problem solving skills?

❑ Will the child have to work alone, or will he participate in group projects, or in front of everyone as she/he reports findings?

❑ How often will major projects come up? Will one grade be given for all participating group members, or will each student get his own grade?

❑ What is the "weight" of projects for final grades?

❑ How much do tests count toward final grades and how are modified tests graded?

❑ How can a student earn extra credit, make up work or substitute a preferred project for one that the rest of the class is working on?

❑ What happens if the student can't keep up? How long will the student have to experience failing grades before modifications (or additional modifications) are made? Who will make this call? How long will it take the parents to even find out that this is happening?

❑ How will the teacher coordinate with the IEP holder to notify her that the student is in trouble because the intensity has become too great?

❑ How will the teachers know if a student is failing one subject, and how long will it take to find out?

❑ If he is failing one class, how does it affect his grade point average toward a final diploma?

There are many questions to ask regarding academics, as you can see, and probably hundreds more that need to be answered. By the time the student graduates from middle school and heads to high school, all of these questions may finally be answered!

Parents will want to work closely with their child's teachers to obtain daily or weekly information on which assignments are due and what work to accomplish each day so that they can help the student in the evenings. Few teachers in middle school are excited about daily or even weekly contact with parents since they have many students, tremendous responsibilities, and no free time to plan for classes. Unlike elementary school, these teachers can see 120 students a day, prepare lessons for all of them, grade hundreds of papers, handle behavior problems and still need to be creative when teaching. It will be exceedingly difficult for them to have a high level of contact with one set of parents. Parents on the other hand, may become depressed thinking that they will never connect with one single person enough to gain the information necessary to help their child complete assignments. Therefore, they may become overly anxious and demanding with their demands on the teacher. This often leads to teacher resistance and high burnout rates.

How do we solve this situation? Don't give up hope; many middle school teachers are willing to go the extra mile and work out arrangements with you when they perceive that the requests are reasonable. It is up to the parent to streamline their requests and find ways for frequent, if not daily contact, without threatening the teacher's short available work time or interfering with her home life.

Middle school teachers, when they have appropriate information and are provided with strategies and training, often go beyond expectations and can surprise even the most jaded parent by being very receptive and gracious about doing everything possible to help your student. Remember that they are in this business because they want to help students (all students) learn and progress. So although you can find some tough middle school teachers out there, don't assume they will all be that way. Give them the benefit of the doubt while you sort through the information you need, set priorities with them, develop a coordinated collaboration system with the school, and streamline your requests in an effort to help your child through these years.

I. Homework Issues and Family Incentive Program

The issue of homework raises its ugly head in middle school for all students, whether disabled or non-disabled. Due to academic intensity, many students take much of their schoolwork home and ask Mom or Dad for help. But at this age, some parents begin floundering because of the many complex issues and abstract concepts that are presented in the middle school curriculum –needless to say, things have changed a lot since the parents went to school. Parents have to keep up with the child's daily work in order to see the relevance between subjects and topics. If they don't keep up they will lose track of the topics presented, and lose track of how one subject relates to another topic that may have been discussed two weeks prior. Does this make parenting difficult? You bet it does!

Along with the acquisition of knowledge, homework increases in proportion as the students prepare for high school. Students with autism/AS that demonstrate significant profiles and cognitive impairment will likely have homework related to functional academics such as reading survival signs, using money in stores, learning daily self-help skills such as cooking, cleaning, sorting laundry, pre-job skills, etc. These skills are just as important to be worked on at home as general education academics. Students who are at higher functioning levels will receive the same amount of schoolwork that the typical students have received. Unfortunately, many of our students who have the capabilities to understand and complete the homework do not do so because of low motivation for the writing or problem solving process. Students with AS may know the topic inside and out, but don't see any reason to prove their knowledge over and over. Subsequently, the student may start balking at homework, causing Mom and Dad to become frustrated and angry, either with the student or the teachers.

Parents who realize that the workload is too heavy for their child must act quickly, before the child becomes so frustrated he "shuts down." This phase may last so long that they eventually drop out of school. Many middle schoolers with autism or AS drop out of school at this time or must be homeschooled whether the parents really want it or not. This happens when parents can't get their child through the school doors in the morning. Before this happens to your child, the parents should call an IEP or Treatment Team Meeting to discuss the workload, and to modify it where necessary. Modifications can be done for the homework assignments, as well as in-class assignments. Please refer back to the previous section on academic modifications.

If parents are struggling trying to get their child to do her homework, they should investigate **positive incentive programming** to provide motivation for task completion. Children can be encouraged to perform multiple assignments with the promise of extra computer time, another television program, time to play or to read. Bedtime snacks are also helpful as an incentive to finish their daily assignments. Parents should be careful to deliver promised rewards and incentives for doing the work or they will likely find their child becoming very resistive to incentive programs. Reinforcers for a positive program must be under total control of the parent, not the student. If the child has unlimited access to the computer or television, he will not work for additional time. Sometimes parents find they must put reinforcers behind a cupboard door and put a lock on it, so that the student does not have access to it. Then, when the student has completed her assignment, she can be given access to the key and allowed into the reward cupboard.

Incentive programs can also be developed around token economy systems, such as earning so many points per page or item of assignment finished, adding to a reward at the end of the night or week, or to build toward a larger purchase. Many of our students love to earn points towards the purchase of action figures, CDs of their favorite music groups, or tickets to attend a favorite movie. (Please refer to Chapter 5 on behavior programming to gather more in-depth details and ideas about setting up an incentive program for the home.)

When setting up an incentive program, parents should ask themselves these questions:

- ❑ What does my child like to do during down time?
- ❑ What kind of ice cream does he like?
- ❑ Where does he like to go outside?

❏   What television programs will he watch?
❏   What is his favorite fast food restaurant?
❏   What music does he prefer?

Obviously, these are just a few questions that can help gain insight into your child's preferences at the moment. However, these preferences change over time, so keep notes or complete a graph, such as the one on page 189 of the Appendix, to help you provide current reinforcers to pair with homework assignments.

A note about students with Asperger's Syndrome

We have mentioned issues about motivation for performance at several points in this book. This is not just an issue for school, but home, too. Students who have this profile often exhibit extremely low motivation for doing any homework whatsoever, and refuse to cooperate with any motivational program that the parent develops. Middle school students with AS can be offended when presented with a program which they feel is demeaning or infantile. They refuse to cooperate, even when the incentives are the strongest possible. They can become very angry at the thought of being "coerced" to do the work through behavior programs, and may exhibit anger or outbursts when moms and dads discuss homework and incentive programs. Parents struggle greatly when this occurs, because they know that their child needs to do the work to maintain their grades. The result for all parties at this point is usually frustration and anger.

The problem with students with Asperger's Syndrome is not that the reinforcers do not motivate them. Rather, it is that there is a much more fundamental issue that they are trying to communicate. Students with AS often do not understand the need for repetition of knowledge. They believe that if they answer the question one time that should be enough for everyone. Teachers, on the other hand, understand that the _typical_ students require much repetition of material before they can cement the knowledge into their long-term memory banks.

Students with AS, however, have phenomenal memories and many times don't require the repetition that teachers assign. Also, students with AS may not understand the need to assimilate the knowledge since it has nothing to do with their particular area of interest. Too, lack of fine motor control among students with this disability usually causes problems with written expression, providing the student with yet another reason to refuse to do the homework assignments. Another reason for lack of motivation for schoolwork can be ascribed to the child's underlying problems with abstract reasoning and problem solving, making assignments confusing and difficult to understand. Middle school academic work calls for more extensive problem-solving abilities and analysis than the student has had to use in elementary school.

Parents and teachers who wish to tackle low performance of homework must first address the underlying issues causing the low motivation. Parents should meet with the teachers to develop a more feasible workload for the student, and investigate options to learn through modification of his academics. Creativity and flexibility in programming is called for in developing more reasonable homework loads for our students with AS. Many benefit from computer assignments, eliminating the need for writing the assignments out. Also, oral testing can replace written tests. Students with AS will benefit by having their teachers and parents develop programs which will highlight and teach them material that does not challenge the very core of their disability and frustrate, confuse and inhibit them. Students with AS can learn tremendously through the years of education even though they pose perplexing problems for their teachers. Parents can help their child understand the family expectations by following through on daily promises and sticking to their guns when rules are set. They can also help by providing the framework for their child to understand that, "Yes, there are some things in life that we all have to do whether we like them or not." You will probably be surprised at how well this works when it is tempered with love and justice.

J. Student Progress Reports

Middle school parents of students with disabilities, by law, must receive notification of their child's grades at least as often as the typical student's parents receive theirs. However, for our students with autism/AS, this may not be enough to keep up with their progress. Also, middle school teachers usually do not coordinate their efforts to monitor how well the student is doing in each of his classes. Therefore, asking one teacher how the student is doing in one class may not yield the information needed. Coordination is required among teachers to obtain a full viewpoint on how they are doing. Unless the IEP holder or parent initiates this, it may not occur.

Students with autism and AS, as well as parents, benefit when they can obtain frequent updates about the student's progress. Information should be provided to parents at least every two or three weeks, but daily information is best. However, teachers may not be enthusiastic about the frequency needed by the parent. Parents must first sit down with the child's teachers and explain the disability to them. It is <u>crucial</u> that they understand the uneven skill patterns which students with autism/AS exhibit and the reason behind the request for daily or weekly information regarding their progress. In this effort, the IEP holder should be able to corroborate the psychological test results and past performance. Middle school teachers will probably not understand this component of the child's disability without having hard facts and performance profiles from the elementary grades.

When requesting frequent contact parents must approach this issue with flexibility. It helps if parents provide teachers with options for contact. Some options that parents can offer include:

❑ Daily phone contact: This will be universally rejected by the teachers (and possibly the parents, as well!) and will quickly lead to both teacher and parent burn-out. It is not wise to choose this option unless the student is in crisis. This option interferes greatly with a teacher's duties, and perhaps even the teacher's personal life and can create negative opinions regarding the student and the parents. Choose this option only if there is no other choice.

❑ Daily journal: Daily written comments by the teacher that the student carries home with him. This option is not universally appreciated either, as it takes the teacher too long to complete. It will be viewed as a teacher-burner, but it does provide a wealth of information.

❑ Daily checklist: As the student leaves each class, he presents the teacher with a list outlining his performance e.g., on a Likert scale of 1-5. The teacher can, without elaboration, make a short notation as to the grade for the day. Then, at the end of every week, each teacher would provide a few sentences of summary as to the student's performance in her own class and the checklist is sent home.

❑ Weekly Performance chart: As in the daily check-list, the teacher could rate the student on a Likert scale of 1-5 and/or an S for satisfactory, which is then sent to the IEP holder at the end of each day. The IEP holder then summarizes the information from the teachers and gives the parents feedback. The student retrieves the form from the IEP holder each morning, carries it all day, and leaves it with his last classroom teacher, who transfers it to the IEP holder. The student can also perform this transfer.

❑ Student self-rating: This is exceptionally important for our students to learn during school years. They will need it for adulthood. McConnell, (1999) states, *"As students complete the self-management sheet, they are learning to monitor and evaluate their own behavior and progress."* Various rating forms exist in school curricula and assessment instruments. Essentially, after each class the student conducts a self-rating form (check-off list) for performance in a number of areas and has the teacher initial the form or change it as necessary. This can either go home every day, or be presented to the IEP holder to summarize. This system is more feasible for the teachers. In addition, it has the advantage of encouraging the student to learn to monitor his own behaviors and performance. Teachers could also provide their own rating in the box if they wish, and then the IEP holder would be able to discuss any discrepancies between them.

❏ <u>Selective daily ratings</u>: As our students have uneven skill development and perform better in some areas than in others, it may not be necessary for the teachers to provide frequent information in all of the student's classes. Choose only the classes that require monitoring and develop one of the above systems to gain information on those classes only. Coursework that is not difficult for a particular student may require only the normal, routine notification of performance levels. Don't forget the social component. Parents may still wish to know how their child is doing socially, even in their best classes, but that can be arranged through other channels.

❏ <u>E-mail correspondence</u>: In this day and age, if a computer can help connect teachers and parents, use it! It may only take a few moments, but can be quite enlightening. Parents, just be very careful not to write volumes, because you then get right back into the problem about being seen as too intrusive.

❏ <u>A final option is treatment team meetings</u>, which are outlined on page 127.

Full-sized examples of charts are available in the Appendix for copying.

Student progress reports can either be time intensive, or must be designed to require minimum time for everyone and yet provide a wealth of information both to teachers and parents. Hopefully, the IEP team will work out the best scenario for providing frequent information to the parents regarding the progress of their student with autism/AS.

K. Attendance Issues and Suspensions

Students with autism/AS who wish to remain on or near grade level academics must maintain solid attendance records. When frequent absences occur, students quickly lose ground academically and will struggle even more to catch up to their peers. Students attending block scheduling classes will fall hopelessly behind if there are frequent absences. Many of our students with this disability have frequent community therapies such as speech therapy, social skills training, occupational therapy, sensory therapy and other community activities. Parents should do their best to make sure that these therapies do not interfere with the student's attendance at school and should eliminate in-school hours for community therapies. Middle school usually determines whether this student remains fully included, or will begin to have increased numbers of pull-out classes. It would be a shame to have teachers view this student as not being able to perform on grade level and sent to resource classes solely because of absences.

Students who have intensive profiles and are receiving community based instruction miss both access to typical peers and valuable instruction when they are not in school. The more experience they have in generalizing the skills learned in the community, the more independent they will be as adults. Therefore, attendance issues are equally important for students along the full spectrum of this disability.

Frequently, behavioral episodes cause absences from school. Teachers or schools may call parents to come and get their child from school because their behaviors have become too severe. Unfortunately this sets a bad precedent, which the student learns quickly. Sending them home for behavioral infractions in the long run is not beneficial to the student or to the school.

The behavioral component is one of the main domains of impairment in students with autism/AS. No one is surprised (nor should they be) when a student with this disability displays inappropriate behaviors. Unfortunately, schools often differentiate between *less* severe behaviors and *more* severe behaviors when they should really be lumped together. Whenever a student displays an inappropriate behavior, regardless of the severity, it should be regarded as an area for instruction and remediation.

Special education teachers are supposed to have learned behavioral techniques to address inappropriate behaviors. If they feel inadequate because of their level of training or the severity of the behavior, then it is their responsibility to seek assistance from their department in addressing these behaviors. Sending a student home for inappropriate behaviors eliminates valuable instruction time and only points out to the parents that the school hasn't a clue how to handle severe behaviors. (Sending the student home for legitimate reasons such as illness or injury is not an issue here.)

School principals may ask about the policy of routine suspension for legitimate infractions of district policies. Yes, schools can and do suspend students for behavioral infractions, and in an inclusive setting our students are viewed as no different than their typical peers. Some states around the country are interpreting IDEA differently because of certain disciplinary practices in inclusive settings.

Behaviors exhibited by students with this disorder are still different from the behaviors of typical students. The inappropriate behaviors exhibited are usually the result of their impairments in communicative understanding and social interactions, as well as a result of low developmental coping skills and low frustration levels. Typical students that have behavior problems do not demonstrate these neurological deficit areas, meaning they have an ability to understand the reasons for the suspensions. Students with autism/AS that demonstrate real deficits and uneven skill patterns usually do not understand a suspension. They may formulate different reasons or lessons from these suspensions than do typical students – they learn that they can have a whole new program which they devise from their behaviors and cannot perceive how this might affect them in the future, or affect their families.

Students with autism that are suspended learn lessons that we would rather they not learn. If you have a student who has been suspended, the first course of action is to call a treatment team meeting or an IEP team meeting immediately to develop a program to address the behavior. This is not a pattern we want to have repeated.

L. Organizational Skills

Students with autism/AS are notorious for their lack of organizational skills. Individuals in society demand this organization from our students – the students themselves do not demand it. Unfortunately, organizational skill goes to the heart of the disability of autism because it ends up as a social affair – pleasing others with how you behave. Folks with this disorder do not have a full appreciation of other people's wants and needs, or they are more isolated and possibly oblivious to the demands of the environment. Students in inclusive settings will probably have great difficulty with the expectations of teachers.

Students with this disability need assistance in this area. Many teachers do not understand that this is an area for *direct instruction*. Sixth grade teachers will attempt to teach organizational skills to our students in the same manner that they do typical students. However, typical students will assimilate these strategies much more readily than students with autism/AS. Again, teachers often become upset and angry with our students because they do not conform to the norm and do not sharpen their organizational skills quickly. This leads to frustration for the student because she does not understand why everyone is getting so upset, and frustration for the teacher who may feel this student is being manipulative and oppositional.

Parents should discuss organizational skills at the IEP in the spring, prior to the student entering middle school in the fall. Teachers should be told directly that this student will need assistance to learn the necessary organizational skills for middle school. Teachers should be designated to help the student check which materials are needed for classes, which ones to take home, and/or which ones must remain in the locker until the correct time. Helpful methods must be found for the student to become independent throughout his day. He must have the material necessary to identify the content, such as color-coded folders or assignment papers, a three-ring binder for each class, or some other visual method easily understood by the student. It is exceedingly unfair to grade a student lower on academics because he can't manage papers or books for the class.

A note: Students with this disorder, especially those with AS who are fully included, may not want visible indicators of assistance. Teachers must be creative in teaching this valuable skill without causing undue attention or embarrassment. Non-verbal cues and messages, which are taught to the student first, can help them learn to adapt their behaviors to the norm without causing the student to become the focus of attention or teasing. Teachers should create subtle signals that can be exchanged across the room indicating that the student understands. Another method is for the teacher to give the student a small list as he enters the classroom. The list shows the materials needed for that class. Token economy systems can be attached to this, whereby the student is awarded a set number of points per class period for adhering to the list. They can then turn in the points at the end of the day to the IEP holder for a small reinforcer, or save them for the end of the week for a larger reinforcer. An example of a form is as follows:

Class Materials List

Date:_____   Day:_____

Class	Which Book is needed?	Got your Notebook?	Turned in Assign?	Got Pen? Sharp pencil?	Stored other	Got extra paper?	What's tonight's books?	Points earned assign?
Period 1								
Period 2								
Period 3								
Period 4								
Period 5								
Period 6								

Check off each box or award points: 0-5

This form can be reduced to the size of a 3 x 5 card or smaller, if necessary. The number of points that the student awards himself for completing each segment can be a prior decision between student and IEP holder and can change over time. Although graphs or check-off lists can be helpful, the student may require extra direct instruction that is conducted by the IEP holder away from the regular education classroom and the prying eyes of the peers. Explanations should be provided to the student as to why she needs to have her books, materials and assignments organized. It is likely you will need to concentrate on teaching routines which the student can learn to follow repetitively. Many students with this disorder may never fully appreciate the reasons behind the need; they need only understand that it is expected of them by all of their teachers. Reinforcement systems should be investigated and attached to these behaviors as they are to other types of behaviors requiring change. Refer to the previous section on motivation to understand the procedures for setting up these systems.

Although we will get into peer programming topics in the next section, it is worth mentioning here in the organizational section that peers can help our students learn these new organizational systems. *Trained* peer tutors can often accomplish much more with the student than teachers. Don't forget to investigate this very useful system when considering teaching organizational skills.

M. Team Teaching

Co-taught, team teaching or collaborative teaching can be very beneficial to our students and is the system upon which many inclusion programs are built. Across this nation, more and more students with disabilities are enjoying access to typical students and a regular school curriculum through a team-taught class. Every parent considering inclusion programming should ask if their school system is using co-taught classes to teach students with disabilities in general education.

Team taught or collaborative-taught classes usually means that in each class used for inclusive programming with students with disabilities, there is a regular education teacher and a special education teacher (not paraprofessional, though an additional aide can be present, as well). As the regular education teacher conducts the lessons, the special education teacher works with any student needing assistance or additional instruction. This is usually the included student but is sometimes the typical students as well, who have stumbled upon a concept they don't understand. By working with any of the students at any time, the typical students often do not realize that she is a "special education teacher," nor which students she is actually assigned to assist.

This arrangement works nicely for our high-functioning folks who do not wish undue attention drawn to them by a "special" teacher. Students with AS sometimes become upset and will refuse the needed support because it points out to the other students that they need help, causing them embarrassment. However, when the teacher rotates among all students, including the ones with AS, the student will not feel so singled out for assistance.

Another method for team taught classes is to have the regular education teacher and the special education teacher co-teach or team teach sections of the content to all students, and frequently change places and duties. Although this works as well as the previous method, it usually means more coordination between the two teachers. It also means routine meetings to plan who will conduct which portion of the content and when. Additionally, this places the regular education teacher in the role of directly instructing the student with the disability and calls upon her knowledge and expertise in the particular disability. She will have to become extremely familiar with the teaching strategies necessary, as well as both familiar and comfortable with implementing any behavior program. This method can work beautifully with two energetic and competent teachers, but can quickly fall apart if they do not maintain that enthusiasm for each other's jobs. Problems can also arise if there are no regular coordination meetings, or if one of the teachers encounters a situation for which she has not been trained. Students with autism/ AS often present us with scenarios that are unique to the teaching realm, challenging untrained teachers.

Another option for co-taught classes is to have the special education teacher substitute entirely for the regular education teacher for one class. This allows the special education teacher to target the included child's instructional needs very specifically, within the context of teaching the regular education students. She can modify the instruction either before or immediately upon presenting it to all the students, thereby meeting her student's needs. This can work beautifully, but it is contingent upon the special education teacher's skill and comfort in teaching core academics, her creativity in spontaneous modification, and on planning time for that one particular class period. Without these components, special education teachers may become mired in the demands of teaching regular academics along with the demands of her own students.

N. Areas of Strength/Splinter Skills

Many of our autism/AS students have areas of high ability; a few will have true splinter skills in one area. Many of our students with this disability meet criteria for gifted or enrichment classes. However, they are often eliminated from gifted classes because they do not meet eligibility criteria across several domains. This is unfortunate because it can eliminate the student from the one area that may, ultimately, keep up their motivation for learning and going to school.

Many students who are high functioning autistic or Asperger's Syndrome drop out of school because they are not motivated in the classwork and cannot seem to enter the accelerated courses. They continue to be placed in classes that are far below their functioning levels due to their poor performance and poor test-taking abilities. Teachers should closely monitor the true levels of functioning for students with this disability and have entrance criteria waived if they feel their student could learn in even one accelerated class.

As adults, students with autism/AS have a good chance of having jobs in their areas of strength. They have true gifts in science, computer, geography and other fact-based courses that can lead to employment in their communities, or to post-secondary learning. Sadly, many are eliminated from the higher classes before they get the opportunity to prove their gifts.

Special education teachers must work overtime with their PR skills and autism information to help their school system and the accelerated teachers recognize the ability levels in our students with autism/AS. Teachers need to understand that this student may still require modifications or accommodations in the course work, even in gifted classes. Just because they have difficulty writing or understanding abstract concepts, they should not be eliminated from higher learning.

Students with AS often burn bridges quickly through their low motivation for course work, behavioral outbursts, non-participatory style and isolative demeanor. Teachers in the accelerated classes may feel that our students don't belong "if they can't behave and do all the work as the others do." Teachers of gifted classes can be teachers who allow creativity, recognizing the unique gifts of our students, or they can be rigid and elitist, believing that only the top performers who adhere to all the stringent requirements of entry belong. Obviously this is an over-simplification. There are many teachers who do, indeed, fit this mold, but many others who are between these two extremes.

It goes without saying that teachers who allow creativity are the ones we want, not just for our students, but for all students. If you have the other type of teacher, then you have the option to demand the rights of the student be followed to get them into these classes. Having them in a class with an unwilling teacher can be a disaster. The situation must be monitored very closely to make sure that the student is accepted and is learning the content.

Teachers must also look outside traditional methods of content delivery if they are to motivate our students with higher abilities who happen to have HFA or AS. Computers can be used extensively to help teach. Many courses can be computer-taught or computer assisted, to the delight of our students with autism/AS. Look beyond the computer as well. Find academic games, outside assignments involving visiting university libraries or public institutions to gather information. Although this is much easier in high school electives, it can also be done in middle school. Students who have higher functioning abilities can achieve greatness when they have their unique gifts targeted and built upon, helping them to turn their intense interests into life-long learning.

Teachers can also help a student be realistic with his strengths. Sometimes, the student's ability levels can open many doors, but their area of interest within that domain may limit their future employment. For example, one young man is very good at reading geography and maps; that is all he really wants to do is to read maps, nothing else. His teachers can steer him to adult employment in cartography by helping him explore maps in more detail. Teaching him survey methods, map reading and scale plotting can all enhance his future employability.

Another example is a young man who loves dinosaurs and wants to be a paleontologist. However, there are few paleontologists in the world; most of them have other jobs, such as teaching in universities or working for large corporations. This student, who has such tremendous strengths in his splinter skills, will need to learn other aspects that he can use as an adult. Working in a museum, for example, or using investigative methods to research dinosaur bones. Although we want him to continue to work toward paleontology, he may very well be eliminated because of his deficit in other areas of functioning.

Focusing on high achieving areas or splinter skills can help us reach a student and give us the road map for helping the student determine his or her life's work. But we sometimes have to help the student transform their interest or skill into realistic goals for their life, and give them pathways to higher learning and real jobs as adults.

7

Social Programming

The art of mastering social skills begins in earnest in middle school. While the foundations of social skills have been learned in elementary school, it is at this next level where social skills are taken to new heights of sophistication.

While social skills are developed in elementary school, the level of skills among middle school typical peers is so much higher making it difficult for our students to keep up. Social programming, therefore, must be a topic for serious discussion at the IEP meeting prior to entering middle school.

Whether the autism/AS student will be fully included, or exposed to typical students for the first time, there are many social growth options for middle school students. Moreover, research has shown the benefits of addressing social interactions for students with autism in the presence of non-disabled peers (Kamps, Leonard, Vernon, Dugan, and Delquadri, 1992; Schleien, Mustonen and Rynders, 1995; Voeltz et al., 1983; Brady et al., 1985; Gaylord-Ross, Haring, Breen, & Pitts-Conway, 1984; and Odom, Hoyson, Jamieson, & Strain, 1985). This should be investigated by all special education teachers to support their efforts in trying to teach these worthwhile skills. Kamps, et al., state,

> . . . *social skills training for students with autism conducted concurrently with nonhandicapped peers was a viable procedure for increasing the frequency of, time engaged in, and duration of social interaction for children in play groups. Perhaps as important were increases in levels of initiations and responses by targets and the responsivity of the peers to targets.*

This style of programming calls for extensive analysis and development of social programs in areas that are not touched upon to this degree for typical students. It also demands training of both teachers and students, and consistent strategies among teachers who have never previously been exposed to the intensity of social programming.

First things first . . .

Before we address fully included students, let us look for a moment to the social needs of students with more intense profiles.

Middle school is "make or break" time for students with autism/AS for access to typical peers. Many don't view students with more severe autism/AS as candidates for inclusive styles of programming because the core curriculum is so intense and rigorous, even for typical students. They believe that inclusive programming will tax cognitive functioning, and they also believe that behavior issues must be addressed differently. I.D.E.A. states quite clearly, however, that the student must be viewed first and foremost as a regular education student. Only then can he be seen as a student with special needs who, for one reason or another, cannot be educated with the general population. If you want social programming close to typical students for your student, then you must discuss this at the IEP meeting and have it written into the document, outlining objectives that will *target specific skills*. Without it, this may not happen.

Today we have many students with autism/AS being educated with no contact with typical students. These students are seen as "special education students" instead of "regular education students with specialized needs." These are two different perspectives. Special education teachers are sometimes more caught up in this rigid way of thinking than others. They have become so accustomed to their students being isolated they do not understand how to do social inclusion at this age, and anything new would change their job descriptions and duties. As a result, you have many students with this disability who have no contact whatsoever with other students in school.

Few of our students eat lunch in schools where they are actually mixed in. Is there a self-contained or segregated McDonald's or Burger King out there? Is there a supermarket in the world that has "special education day" just for our students to shop? Of course there isn't, and we must not teach our children to live in a world that doesn't exist.

Special education teachers must forge new ground in their own schools and broach the subject of social introduction to typical students. In the real world, CEO's work beside senior and junior administrative assistants and janitors. In very few jobs do people work alone. If special education teachers do not broach the idea of having, for example, an integrated lunch with the typical peers, then more inclusive ideas will fall by the wayside. It will then be much harder to gain administrative or teacher support for true inclusive styles of programming.

Many special education teachers are at the forefront of their profession and are already investigating and setting up many of the programs that will be outlined in this chapter. Students with greater needs can also benefit by exposure to typical students. Such exposure will help prepare students for their adult lives when special teachers will not be hovering over their every need.

You may decide to begin your social inclusion program with your students who are more severely autistic, or you may choose those with less severe profiles. Whichever you pick, do not begin the students' exposure without the proper training and support that is needed for success. Much planning and development must go into this programming in order to help the student succeed and benefit. *Inclusion programming does not, under any circumstances, mean "dumping"!* It also doesn't mean that inclusion is about being *like* everyone else—it means only *alongside* everyone else. Do not jeopardize your program and your student's mental and physical well being by implementing a program that is thrown together. Research your program thoroughly. Use the Internet to look up peer programming, social skills, inclusion, tutoring or mentoring programs, etc. Obtain other books that might help you in formulating the best program possible. Teachers and parents should come to the IEP meeting well prepared to offer ideas and suggestions and strategies for developing the best program for this particular student. Parents in their excitement or impatience often want this stage to go quickly – but don't skip the development phase of this process in the rush to gain the access to typical peers, for you will likely regret it.

Individuals who are "high-functioning"

What about the students with high functioning autism or Asperger's Syndrome? These students are often in need of social intervention but have been left to drift because they are able to keep up academically, and because their social needs are not recognized. When this happens, students with this profile may exhibit depression, loneliness, and vulnerability because they want friends, don't know how to get them, and may be open to mimicking inappropriate behaviors of the peers in order to gain their friendships. Unfortunately, the behaviors of mimicked peers may not be behaviors the parents want imitated.

Social programming is a must when considering *any* student with autism/AS, regardless of the severity of profile. Remember, social impairment is one of the largest, indeed many will say the main, deficit area for someone with autism/AS. To ignore this domain is to ignore one-third of the disability and can hamper an individual in ways that are unforeseen.

Please consider the following sections when you are beginning to develop a social program for your child or student with autism/AS.

A. Peer Tutor Programs

For years teachers at all levels have used formal peer tutor programs for academic assistance. Research has documented the benefits of this method, both for disabled and non-disabled students (Sprague, J., & McDonnell, J. 1986), Burrell, B, Wood, S. J., Pikes, T., Holliday, C., (2001). Peer tutor programs at the middle school level are more rare, though just as necessary. They can be developed for either the student who is fully included, or for the student who is included for one or two classes only. (Peer tutoring programs can also be used to start reverse mainstreaming programs, i.e., programming students from regular into special education classes. Since this book highlights the more inclusive styles of programming, however, we will not look deeply into programs for special education classes. It is sufficient to know they can be very useful.)

Peer tutor programs are not new to middle school, but they are certainly not used for students with autism to the extent they are in elementary schools. Many teachers use peer programming for academic reasons and these programs are integral to their teaching style. Teachers do not consider formal peer tutoring programs in middle school simply because of the nature of the typical middle school student. Middle school students have the capability of being compassionate and helpful one moment and absolute fiends the next, and middle school teachers recognize this. Teachers may feel the students are too volatile or immature to be asked to model for others. This will make it tougher for the special education teacher who wishes to convince regular education teachers to try her program and why peer programming for social skills must by necessity rely on the more mature student.

Pairing a typical student with a student with autism to help increase social skills is exceedingly important in middle school. Students with autism/AS require social programming through peer tutoring programs simply because one-third of their disability is lack of social skills. Also, as this student has aged into the middle school years, they probably retain learned behaviors which may be deemed inappropriate to the social world of their age-mates.

Peer tutor programs for social skills must be carefully conducted in an inclusive setting. Choosing the wrong peer to tutor the student with autism/AS can be devastating if the peer teases or victimizes the student. Conversely, choosing the right peer can help the student with autism/AS build friendships and confidence in academic and social performance.

Qualities to look for in a peer include:

- Calm personality: a person who is not easily thrown by unusual reactions or answers to questions.
- Sense of humor: having humor can help the student with autism/AS learn how to appreciate jokes and idioms that are used by age-mates and learn the latest jargon used by the peers.
- Ability to understand the academic content and teach it to someone else when called upon. Social instruction can be taught in the midst of academic tutoring, as well.

- Ability to deflect teasing by others: This person should be able to handle him/herself when teased by others, so that they can model the strategies used to deflect teasing or protect the student with autism/AS from being teased. Someone who can deflect the teasing without having it escalate into troublesome situations.
- Move easily among peers: This person should be able to move within the confines of the typical social network without creating enemies, or setting age-mates against each other. If possible, this person should be "popular" among peers.
- Have many stable friends: With stable friends, this person can offer introduction to other peers outside of the classroom setting.
- Not easily swayed by the fads, such as ones that may cause the student to experiment in drugs, sex, violent themes, etc. However, since these topics are openly discussed among peers at this age, parents of the student with autism/AS should be prepared for questions surrounding these issues.
- Consistency in personality: Although this may be difficult at this age, it is best to find a peer who does not regularly swing from one extreme to the other with their moods. Someone that generally tempers their personality with insight and realistic expectations of themselves and others.

In short, we are looking for a mature, stable, intelligent, compassionate, and articulate, sociable person.

Is it possible to find such a person at this age? It will be difficult to find this wonderful peer tutor as you may find several students that fit some of the qualifications, but not all. Obviously, it is better to find students who can fit some of the requirements than to choose someone that meets none of them. Ask for the assistance of other teachers to help you select the appropriate peers for your student with autism/AS. Look to honors programs or gifted classes where students may be more mature.

After assembling a list of candidates, discuss the option of being a peer tutor with each student, and then with their parent. Get the parents' view of their child. Ask the parents (as well as teachers and friends) if they believe this person has "the right stuff" to make the long-term commitment to tutoring, mentoring and guiding a fellow student with special educational and social needs.

Once a peer or peers has been chosen to act as a social tutor for the student with autism/AS, it is wise to gain the _written_ permission of their parents to participate in the program. Send the parents a letter that outlines the mission, goals and objectives of the program, as well the requirements of the job. Make sure that the parents send the letter back for your records. A sample letter follows and this letter can be easily modified. If this student will also act as an academic tutor, the letter can be modified to include subject material, classroom strategies, times of tutoring, etc.

Dear Parents,

(Student's name) has been selected to participate in a special program designed to assist students with disabilities in your school. This program will provide assistance to students with social skills needs.

(Student's name) was identified and selected by a team of teachers because of his/her skills and abilities, his/her ease with fellow classmates, and his/her warm, caring and outgoing personality.

In order for (student's name) to participate in this program, we must have your permission. He/she will be paired with a student with a disability during portions of the day to act as a model of strong social skills. He/she will also help this student interact socially with other students. He/she may be asked to sit alongside the student at lunch time to talk and introduce them to others. She/he may also help them transition from class to class, invite them to after-school activities on occasion, and generally help pave the way, socially, for a student in need. No academic time will be compromised for your student, nor should academic grades be affected at all.

This program strictly targets social skills and we hope (student's name) will form a strong bond with the student with whom they have been paired, and that this student will learn appropriate social behavior from your child.

Peer tutoring is a long-standing program to teach better and more appropriate skills to students with disabilities. We hope that you will allow your child to participate in this worthy program and that they, too, will learn from the experience.

Please complete the bottom portion of this letter and return it to your child's homeroom teacher. We thank you for your consideration of this program and would be happy to answer any questions that you may have. We can be reached at: _____.

Student's Name: _____

Grade _____ Homeroom Teacher: _____

Parent's Name: _____

Address: _____

Phone Number: _____

I give my permission for my child to be a peer tutor: _____Yes _____ No

Parent Signature/Date: _____

Once peers have been chosen and permission granted, they will require training. Do not expect them to automatically understand everything. At this age, middle school students want to learn more about the disability and will ask lots of questions such as; why the student needs help, if the disability is contagious, and if the disabled student ever gets better. Explanations in elementary school are much easier and many times the title "autism" or "Asperger's Syndrome" is not mentioned at all. At that age, telling the peer buddies that the child "has a boo-boo on the brain" is enough.

That explanation won't cut it in middle school. Be prepared to talk a little about the disorder of autism if asked to, but do not provide unlimited technical information. Discuss major areas of impairment, as well as the particular disabilities of the student to which they have been assigned. Discuss different situations that may arise, how to handle them, how to deflect or redirect inappropriate comments or questions, and how to form their own language into sentences that can best be understood by someone with this disorder. Discuss the problems with abstract reasoning, the inability to understand witty comments or jokes, and what to tell the student when they are perceived as doing something embarrassing for a middle school student.

Finally, be sure to discuss what they should do when they encounter a situation or problem which they cannot handle. Let them know when, how and from whom to seek help and assistance. Be sure to foster an atmosphere of open dialog among the tutors and the teachers.

The biggest mistake made in peer programs is believing that the peer tutor can go it alone for the rest of the year, with little intervention from the teacher. That can and does create problems when working with peer tutors. Because autism/AS is such a confusing diagnosis, your tutors will require continual training throughout the year. Schedule routine meetings among the tutors and the teachers so that a network is established, questions are answered, and updated information and strategies are disseminated. Schedule these meetings during the day, perhaps during homeroom time, so that the tutors do not miss any classes. It is also helpful to have the school counselor attend, if possible, to assist in answering questions. Once-a-month meetings can go a long way towards maintaining enthusiasm for the project. If necessary, or if important information needs to be distributed, schedule meetings more frequently.

Give your peer tutors reinforcement. They are spending their free time with this assigned student and should receive recognition for it. (Please see Credited Peer Programs on page 113.) Other methods of recognition should be investigated, such as letters of commendation sent to the parents or put in the students school records, occasional notes left for them that they are doing a good job, small treats, etc. Teachers naturally reinforce students as part of their teaching style and reinforcing peer tutors should not be alien to them.

It would be wonderful if our students with autism/AS could learn social skills naturally in an environment where everyone was included in all aspects of learning. When working with students with autism/AS, however, it is apparent from their level of disability that they do not as easily absorb social skills as do typical students. They usually require both direct and incidental instruction in necessary skills needed for appropriate social functioning.

Students with autism/AS who have reached middle school age and still require instruction in social skills have proven that they have not absorbed these needed skills from the elementary grades or from family members. If they are to learn the social skills necessary for a higher level of independence in their adult lives, we must address this issue now. We cannot wait until the high school years when the child is even further behind socially.

During the middle school years, we must use every known method to help students with autism/AS learn skills that will lead to increased social independence. We must do this before they move on to high school, where the emphasis will be on moving these skills into the wider world of adulthood, and later into employment opportunities. Once they reach the adult years, training opportunities are scarce.

So, should we use peer tutor programs?

How you answer that question depends strongly on the student's profile of autism or AS. But I strongly encourage parents and teachers to consider this style of programming to supplement and assist the individual and incidental instruction of social skills.

Peers can help the student generalize learned skills into their social world far better than we adults can. Typical middle schoolers, unfortunately, are not likely to take on the task without encouragement and leadership from both teachers and parents. Peer tutor programs should be discussed, at the very least, at the IEP and/or treatment team meetings.

B. Social Skills Objectives for the IEP

Many professionals feel that social impairment is the largest problem area for someone with autism. Yet many students with autism/AS in middle school do not have the social domain addressed at all.

Social objectives in IEP's usually cover the topics of "following classroom rules," or not "being aggressive toward anyone." They do not target positive social initiations and responses between or toward their age-mates. Examples of social skills objectives commonly seen are: (taken from real IEP's)

_____ will reduce his negative interactions with others by refraining from hitting or pinching.

_____ will sit appropriately next to a peer during class time.

_____ will increase his appropriate social behaviors.

_____ will learn identify of self.

_____ will learn to appreciate her own bodily space and the personal space of others.

_____ will adjust their behavior to the expectations of others.

These objectives are not social *interaction* goals, nor are they even *measurable*. (The author continues to puzzle over the definition of "identify of self." What do you suppose this means?) Social interaction goals are few and far between. Yet it is difficulty interacting with people or socially inappropriate behaviors in front of others that often gets our folks into trouble.

Definitions of social skills vary. A student must maintain appropriate behaviors while in an inclusive setting and will need IEP objectives that address developing positive behaviors to replace inappropriate ones. The problem arises when objectives address only socially inappropriate behaviors, and not socially interactive behaviors. Without interactive behaviors, the student will learn to control angry behaviors but never learn to participate in a conversation, share in games or activities, or coordinate eye contact with requests to play. Simply suppressing behaviors is not enough; we must teach new behaviors as well. Parents and teachers should consider the following social interaction skills when writing IEP objectives for the social domain.

_____ will greet 2 peers each morning with "good morning."

_____ will remain within 3 feet of peers during activities in the classroom.

_____ will initiate interaction with peers at least 3 times per day.

_____ will respond to a peer's initiation by making eye contact and listening to the entire question or statement asked.

_____ will state, "it is my turn" in a quiet voice to a peer when working in a cooperative group.

Social skills are absolutely necessary for any student with autism or Asperger's Syndrome. In middle school, with the focus on academics, social skills training is viewed as unnecessary for typical students. But unless social skills are taught directly to autism/AS students, it is unlikely they will reach mastery in these areas during the middle school years. By the middle school years, unfortunately, students with autism/AS usually have deep-rooted inappropriate behaviors that they have carried from the elementary years. These behaviors will require constant attention to change.

C. Social Skills Assessment

Middle school students may still have inappropriate behaviors which have either proven resistant to remediation or were not addressed previously. Therefore, you will need to begin somewhere in addressing and setting priorities for IEP objectives. But where do you start?

The first step is to obtain a solid social skills assessment.

There are many social skills assessments on the market. An excellent one that should be investigated is the Walker-McConnell Scales of Social Competence and School Adjustment (Walker, McConnell, 1995). The Walker-McConnell is a normed instrument based on a Likert scale which provides the teacher with standard scores referenced to typical development. This and other normed instruments look not only at basic social skills, but also at pragmatic language skills (social and language skills go hand-in-hand, especially in the upper ranges of this disorder), and classroom behaviors. By conducting assessment, the teacher and parent will have an excellent profile of the student's appropriate social behaviors.

There are many other social skills assessment instruments besides the ones mentioned. Some may be based upon Likert scales (0-5) but not normed. Others are narratives which provide anecdotal evidence of levels of social behaviors. School counselors usually have access to a wide variety of instruments through school catalogs and educational publishers. Many of these routine instruments do not get to the depth of analysis that our students with autism require, so schools should ask for a publisher's review copy and select carefully.

A social skills assessment should be conducted two or three times during the first year: once at the beginning of the year, at the end of the school term, and if possible at the mid-point to provide any required mid-course corrections and modifications to the IEP objectives. During the second year, it should only be necessary to conduct the assessment at the mid-point and end of the year. You will have the previous end-of-year measure to use for the beginning of the fall term as the objectives have been based upon those scores.

Examples of social skills from an assessment instrument (Walker-McConnell) include the following:

- Relates well to the opposite sex
- Takes pride in her/his appearance
- Makes friends easily with others
- Does what he/she agrees to do
- Accepts constructive criticism from peers without becoming angry
- Has a sense of humor
- Listens while others are speaking

These items are still not truly measurable and thus cannot be used directly in an IEP, but dozens of measurable objectives can be based upon the needed skill identified as deficient for your student.

Students with autism/AS require the social skills objectives -basic fact. Don't leave home without them.

D. Direct Instruction of Social Skills

At the middle school level, direct instruction of social skills takes on new meaning.

In the lower grades, direct instruction was easily done individually or in small groups, with ready acceptance from the typical peers. In middle school, however, if small groups are used for direct instruction, then peers must be carefully selected to prevent sabotage of the group (see the definition of appropriate peers described previously). It is also harder to find times of the day when peers and the autism/AS student can be pulled out of class to participate in the small group. Teachers (and parents) may object if their students miss any portion of the day's lessons to address these concerns. Therefore, other options must be explored to teach needed social skills. The following suggestions may be helpful for both teachers and students.

- Individual sessions with the school counselor during homeroom, speech time.
- Independent or elective course used to teach an academic subject meshed with social skills.
- Individual sessions with the special education teacher during resource time.
- After-school sessions with the speech teacher or special education teacher, if possible.
- Community groups/therapy; may be found at local hospitals, in combination with OT/ Rehab services; speech schools.
- Local psychologist who can offer social skills training as part of therapy.

E. Choosing a Social Skills Curriculum

Once the time has been determined, the teacher or facilitator must identify which curriculum will be used to teach social skills. There are many excellent ones on the market. Also, many school systems already have effective curricula that they use to teach character education, and these can be used for the direct instruction sessions. However, don't rely on curricula that address anger management. Our students with autism/AS need more than that.

Items to look for in evaluating a social skills curriculum include the following topics (they may have some or all of these components):

❏ Skills connected to developmental milestones
❏ Concrete definition of each skill
❏ Wide range of social skills addressed
❏ Both basic and sophisticated levels of social skills addressed, from eye contact (basic) to handling embarrassment (sophisticated)
❏ Rating forms connected to the curriculum (see the next section in case they don't have this component) including both teacher and self-rating forms
❏ Suggested activities to use in the sessions
❏ Visual materials suggested to help emphasize the skill
❏ Videotapes to help teach the skill
❏ Role playing methods used
❏ Methods to generalize the skills across settings
❏ Possibilities of adding incentive plans to the system
❏ Concrete suggestions to the teacher on how to run the sessions
❏ Repetitive teaching strategies used to cement the skill

Before a teacher purchases a social skills curriculum, she should investigate many to ensure they are applicable to students with autism. Often they are not, simply because the curriculum assumes that the child has a higher level of social understanding, or because the curriculum defines social skills as teaching students not to engage in school violence.

Students with autism/AS are truly puzzled by the social world and do not understand how other people manage to make friends, analyze the social environment, or adjust their social responses to social input. Therefore, study the curriculum to make sure that the skills are broken down into parts that are feasible for someone with this disorder, and that they are concretely stated. Think about taking a multi-dimensional skill (social skills) and making it *one-dimensional* (concrete; on paper). Keep this in mind when you investigate a social skills curriculum.

Once you have the curriculum, decide how it should be taught: individually, or with one or two peers to help. For young elementary students, small groups can accomplish much in the way of social skills instruction. However, once you get into middle school, you may have to re-examine this in light of the particular profile of your student.

Students with Asperger's Syndrome may not wish to have their direct lessons with their peers and may be embarrassed about having to perform the routines of direct instruction in front of their peers. If that is the case, keep the group small for social activities and games which use incidental instruction rather than direct instruction. If the student has a more pronounced impairment of autism, then direct instruction can be accomplished either individually, or in groups with peers. Most likely, both strategies should be used to increase the effectiveness.

When conducting the social skills session, specific goals should be established. Particular social objectives are chosen based on an assessment of the student. The skill is then defined and examined in light of the student's abilities and past performance. The student should practice the desired skill.

Different scenarios should be created and the student given the chance to perfect new alternatives to previous behaviors. Videotaping responses can be quite useful to the student in self-analyzing his performance and gaining feedback from the teacher/counselor.

F. Student Cliques

Typical students at the middle school age often form cliques which can be either a benefit or a detriment to our students in inclusive classes. Students with autism in middle school are bereft of the very social skills we are trying desperately to teach them. This lack of social skills leaves them vulnerable to outside influences of the typical peers. Typical peers who wish to victimize a student will find ingenious ways to do it when the teacher is not watching. Unfortunately, at this age, typical students have learned the *power* of the non-verbal methods of communicating with one another. They can use it against each other, or against those who don't fit their self-established ideas of "cool." Unstructured times during the school day—between classes, after-school, times when the teacher has been called from the room, etc.—are times when problems with cliques arise.

So how can we keep our students from being targeted by cliques operating in the middle schools? By eliminating all possibility that it will occur by removing our students? Absolutely not! That does not solve our problem or teach skills. Rather, it just wastes time and delays solving the problem. Many parents are terrified by the victimization that can occur at this age, with good reason. We can easily begin to think that even more pullout classes would be better than to let the child be teased or bullied. Sadly, this does occur and is sometimes necessary. But that attacks the problem at the end – not at the beginning. By starting at the beginning and enlisting the support of sympathetic cliques and training them, it is not usually difficult to turn this situation around. And when provided with information, many middle schoolers willingly volunteer to assist any teacher working with them.

When the autism profile of the student is severe, most typical students immediately understand the need for support. However, it is more difficult to gain supporters when the student with autism or AS has milder characteristics, because they look so "typical" in so many ways, and because the behaviors exhibited are often interpreted as manipulative, mischievous, "nerdy," "a pain," and oppositional. Therefore, the teacher who is including students with HFA and AS may need to directly enlist the support of typical students, explain the disorder, train them on methods of redirecting and modeling, and help them understand why this particular student needs help. During the training of these peers, they will also need to be told that part of their duties is to "protect" this student from other, non-supportive cliques, especially during transition times and non-teacher observed times. With these confederates, the student with HFA or AS will not only gain the strong models needed to learn the needed social and language skills, but will also gains friends who can deflect any teasing or targeting from other students.

It is unfortunate that we must sometimes take steps to "protect" students with disabilities who are being included in general education classrooms. In many middle schools (some will say most), it is unneeded. However, the fact remains that in all too many schools, students with HFA and AS in particular are misunderstood and placed in situations that make attending school an ordeal. The wise teacher will be aware of this possibility and will integrate her students into the student body quickly through peer programs before trouble ensues.

It is very important not to point this student out to the entire student body. After all, we want to mesh him into the wider student population. Choosing a small, select group of peers to help and support the student can mean the difference between success and failure in middle school.

G. Credited Peer Programs

Across this nation, many high schools have developed courses for Peer Facilitators, Peer Tutors, and Teacher Cadets which can be helpful to the special education teacher looking at inclusion programming. Teacher Cadet Programs are usually found in some high schools and are meant to help the future teacher learn about the job. Some cadets choose the special education department and can offer valuable assistance to the teacher. Accredited peer programs have also recently been moving into the middle schools. These programs usually have a course outline, a syllabus and approval from the school district as meeting the criteria for accreditation.

Teachers interested in beginning an accredited peer course will need to research the subject to provide a full description of the benefits predicted. Areas to outline include the following:

❏ which students are selected as peers
❏ how the students will be graded
❏ who will supervise the students
❏ how often the student meets with his faculty representative
❏ the entire course syllabus
❏ how much time is spent training
❏ what elective or exploratory class is substituted for the peer facilitation course
❏ how this class fits into the roster of other classes offered
❏ how students will be recruited
❏ what data will be collected
❏ how outcome data will be analyzed and presented

There are probably many other topics which school systems must research before they are persuaded to offer peer facilitation courses in their school. However, once it is established special education teachers will have a range of peers who can help students be included in many ways.

For example, when beginning to consider inclusion, one teacher in a self-contained, special education classroom, used this method to give her students role models for every class, interacting with her students in a reverse mainstreaming pattern. Once that process began, the program was expanded. Peer facilitators can assist the student in regular education classes, sitting alongside, directing and cueing the student. Peer facilitators can be used at lunchtime, sitting and eating with the student and introducing them to other peers.

One teacher spent considerable time developing her program. She presented the program to the school board, explaining the goals and objectives of the program. At the end of the school term or trial period, she took supporting data to present to the school board, along with some of the peers that took the class, their parents, and the parents of the students with autism/AS. She had with her both objective data and anecdotal evidence that the program was a benefit to the school and it was made a permanent class. This was a solid program that opened many doors for the students, the school and the community.

Peer facilitators can open doors for our students with autism/AS, as well as for others who experience disabilities. They are well worth the time and effort of the special education teacher to develop and implement. Accredited peer classes help increase the typical student's awareness of the world and his tolerance for those with different abilities. It also increases acceptance of the child with disabilities by the enrolled peer's friends, family members and others in the community by providing them with a more realistic view of society.

H. Extracurricular Activities

Students who are included with typical peers for coursework should also have the opportunity to attend a range of extracurricular activities. Middle schools vary widely in extracurricular activities. Some middle schools offer none; others offer dozens of activities, both sports-related and academic. Examples of activities include the routine basketball, softball, football, etc., but also drama club, computer club, chess club, gaming club, environmental clubs, various language clubs, school yearbook, academic team, internet newspaper, cheerleaders, Beta and honors clubs, builder's club, dance team, and many others.

Many of these have been borrowed from high school, but are showing up in more and more middle schools. Any interested teacher can form a club as long as there is sufficient supervision of the club and it is sanctioned by the school. In one school, a teacher put out a notice for a new chess club and got over 100 students signed up, then needed to round up more teachers to help supervise, as the initiating teacher had no idea that there was this much interest in the school for chess!

Students with autism/AS who wish to join an extracurricular activity should make sure that they first have the special education teacher support their efforts to break this new ground. First, the teacher should help the student define interest areas, then analyze the reasons for their interest. If they are interested in computers, do they like to play one particular game? If that is true, then the other students will quickly tire of a single game. It would be wise to develop a behavior program for your student in which he must play a range of games first, while interacting with the other students, before being allowed to become focused on his favorite game during club time.

The special education teacher should consider before or after school activity as just another class the student is taking. In other words, all the considerations for structure, instructional levels, make-up of peers, environment, behavior programming, teacher training and peer programs will also apply. You will need a sympathetic and knowledgeable supervising teacher who can assume the same role as a classroom teacher does to ensure behavior programming is continued, to encourage and motivate, and to teach the student new content. She must also make the club appear more informal and less class-like to the attending students. Without these components in place, an extracurricular activity can be just as disastrous as a routine class when not properly supported.

Extracurricular activities are an important component to a school program for any middle school student, whether they are typical or disabled. Make the most of the middle school inclusion project by considering these wonderful opportunities to engage in peer relations and build strong social and language skills.

I. Friendships

All parents of middle schoolers want their children to have strong and lasting friendships with appropriate peers. This is no different for the parents of the students with autism/AS than it is for parents of typically-developing students. Even for typical students, making friends can be difficult during the turmoil of adolescence. For students with autism/AS, making friends is even more difficult. Many students with this disorder understand the definition of "friends" but do not, honestly, understand how you gain and keep them. Many students with Asperger's in particular know that they have no friends and try desperately to find some, often attaching themselves to one group after another that shuns them until they either find their niche, or get lost trying.

When working with this disorder, we must also admit that many students with autism will not have the same concept or meaning of "friendships" that non-autistic individuals have. Plenty of individuals with autism enjoy being around people and will seek them out, but some students with autism will not. Unfortunately, the very definition of a "friend" goes to the heart of social skills, which is a large deficit area for our students with autism/AS. Although they may not understand what a true "friend" is, this does not mean that we should not help them learn about the rich environment of friendships and what wonderful experiences can be shared when you have a friend.

We can teach our students about activities that involve other people, and that activities are more fully enjoyed with other people; we can teach them how to be full, contributing members of activities, thereby offering them the opportunity to engage in these same activities with others. We can also teach them how to talk to others in a socially appropriate manner as well as how to behave in different settings around other people.

We can demonstrate and explain different emotions and how to switch from one to another in socially acceptable ways. We can teach turn-taking, sharing, and how to participate in group academics. Finally, we can teach our students what reciprocity means when talking to others.

Teaching a student how to gain a friend is like taking a society and stripping it of the complexities, breaking it into the various components and making the whole thing one-dimensional and very concrete. Difficult? Yes! Impossible? We hope not, but with some students with autism/AS, it may seem that way.

It is always easier to do this in the elementary grades since elementary schools retain more of the social element in teaching (at least in the lower grades) than middle schools do. It seems as if middle schools favor a strict academic schedule, trying hard to eliminate any social interactions between students. However, as schools have learned the ramifications of poor social skills among their populations (as evidenced by school fights, gangs, shootings, etc.), administrators have begun to incorporate more and more social subjects into their classes.

Effective curricula, social "word of the week" programs, buddy programs and others that target increased acceptance of each other, as well as increased numbers of school counselors on-site mean that schools are now recognizing the need for social guidance for all students. This awareness of the need for social training means increased acceptance among the school administration for creative programs which can help to teach students with autism/AS.

Learning skills and making friends is not the same thing, but the one must precede the other. Making friends must also address generalization of skills across settings. When helping a student with autism/AS build a friendship, peers that live in their own neighborhood should be targeted first, since you want your student to be able to spend time with them outside school as well as inside. Wouldn't it be wonderful for the student to be able to ride to a football game with a friend in the neighborhood? Wouldn't it be wonderful to have your student meet his friend in the local mall and "hang out" or go to a movie together? Those of us in special education often see our elementary students riding the bus for over an hour because they are bused across town for a "special program." But in middle school, students come from a larger geographical setting, offering a better chance that your student will, indeed, be attending with his neighborhood peers. This will take some detective work on the part of the teacher to find these students and to help build a friendship with an age-mate, but it is well worth the effort.

How do you start to build a friend for your student?

First, look to common interest areas. What topic or activity fascinates your student? Cartoons? Computers? Running? Individual sports? Video games? History? It will be much harder to build a friendship around some subjects such as washing machines or trains, since most typical peers will not be fascinated with them as much as your student appears to be. However, conducting an interest inventory can possibly identify other areas of interest that may capture a typical peer's attention. If you do not find a subject, this will be the starting point for you to teach your student new activities.

Assess any and all before- or after-school activities. Choose one or two that you can teach to your student first, so that she can then join that group. Before the student is placed into this group, the teacher should attend a few sessions to meet the students and gain a preliminary feel for the other participants. Friendships can't be formed without proximity, so look for potential "friends" who might be already attending the activity.

After the students have met and begun the process of building an acquaintanceship and then a friendship, the teacher should analyze how the student is doing within the group. Middle schoolers have very definite ideas about forms of talking, dressing, acting, etc. The teacher can absorb some of this knowledge to teach her student during other times, such as during individual social sessions. Peer tutors can help role model and teach the student.

After friendships have begun to form, the teacher can orchestrate other social gatherings during the day that place the two students close together, such as lunch, before school, after school, in the media center, and so on.

What if your student bonds with another student with this same disorder? Is it wrong? Do we only target typical students? This is a tough question to ask and to answer. In inclusive settings, we very much want our students to be able to learn from strong social and language models and it is quite clear that our students with this disability are not great models. Therefore, we target typical students. By middle school, however, students with autism and AS in particular often know that they are different from the typical peers; they feel lost in the social arena, and can become quite severely depressed because they feel so alienated from their peers.

When two students with AS come together at this age, they may have much in common and are surprised to have found someone that understands what they are going through. They can share their thoughts about their particular disorder, commiserate about the horrible setting of middle school and academics, and can generally support each other through this very difficult time. Do we stop them from having this friendship? No, but the wise teacher will monitor the friendship to ascertain what each is learning from the other in the way of aberrant behaviors. It is not wise to keep two friends separated when they can support each other through this difficult time of adolescence. But it is also not wise to allow a relationship to grow when one student is victimized. Learning inappropriate behaviors will make it even more difficult for them to function in society. Teachers must judge this budding friendship from an objective viewpoint and make a decision regarding fostering the relationship or redirecting it.

8

Collaborative Roles

The death knell of many inclusion programs can sometimes be directly linked to the lack of collaboration among the various components of the core program.

Woods (1998) states:

> *Collaboration among teachers, parents, and other school professionals has been recognized as a critical feature of success.*

Unfortunately, by the time most people finally understand the importance of this component, the program is in crisis and teachers and parents are in adversarial roles. In middle school, collaboration is crucial to the benefit derived from the overall program for the student. In elementary school collaboration was so much easier – you usually only had one teacher, one special education teacher, one or two therapists and the parents. Daily and weekly collaboration among all the players was quite easy. Many parents and teachers were happy to talk on a daily basis when Mom came to pick up Junior.

But in middle school, you now have five teachers minimum, plus one or two special education teachers, lead teachers, any number of therapists (both at school and in the community), plus the parents. And, just so that we can make it that much more difficult, the five regular education teachers can change at the end of grading periods! Collaboration among all these parties can be a nightmare. So how can collaboration be accomplished in this hectic, closed society we call middle school?

A. The Program Manager

Collaboration can be accomplished through much effort on the part of the Individual Education Plan (IEP) holder. This is not an easy job and no parent should assume otherwise. In some cases it is an impossible job. The IEP holder must become the program manager, the one person that knows everything about this student throughout the school term. Many times, this person is a teacher of a self-contained classroom or resource teacher who has established caseloads of other students, with the inclusion students added to her roster. She will find it difficult to find the time to meet with all of the teachers, obtain lesson plans from them all, pre-teach or post-teach lessons, and do all the other time-consuming things that keep the program going. She must truly be a master of all her domain. Many special education teachers can master this role; many can't.

If the IEP holder is not an "organized" person, then she will quickly have to learn how to efficiently manage an inclusion program for a student with this disability. She should pinpoint areas of need for herself before organizing the student's program so that she has a better view of her time and capabilities. There is nothing wrong with asking for assistance from the regular education teachers regarding the development of the program. She will be faulted by others if she does not recognize the need to have everything organized from the beginning of the year. Therefore, the IEP holder should:

- get an objective viewpoint of her own skills from friends, relatives, supervisor, principal, etc. (As in behavior programming, start with yourself first. Make up your own form to gather their opinions if you must, just so you can view your own skills through the eyes of others.);

- review all materials on the student before the school year begins;

- have parents or past teachers complete the portfolio form at the end of this book;

- meet with all of the teachers that will have the student for the first grading period;

- analyze and set schedules of paraprofessionals;

- develop collaboration materials (forms) that will be used on a daily/weekly basis;

- gather materials on the disability to give to the teachers;

- meet with the parents to discuss concerns and likely transition problems;

- meet with the student (if she does not already know him) to help allay any fears;

- set meeting schedules for the first 9 weeks so that teachers can plan ahead and reserve time;

- get some sleep; you're going to need it!

The program manager can "make or break" a program, depending on how well she is organized. If she is disorganized, then the regular education teachers will be discussing it in the teacher's lounge, passing negative opinions to the next set of teachers who have this student. This will be devastating to the student simply because he will be looked on as a "troublemaker," and will not be given much leeway behaviorally. It is much more difficult to come back from this position than if it had gone smoothly in the beginning.

Predictably, this scenario puts great pressure on the IEP holder. It is wise for the administrators to understand this and support this person in whatever way they can, to provide resources to the teacher, to accompany her to meetings, and to generally provide her with the knowledge that she is well-supported by them. This can mean the difference between job satisfaction and burn-out.

B. Between Home and School

Collaboration between home and school during the middle school years is quite different from the elementary years. Parents may feel that they are suddenly lost, that they no longer have control over their child's program, and that their opinion is not heeded in the face of so many teachers. This must be prevented at all costs.

Middle school teachers are not used to providing a high level of day-to-day information to parents, and will be very surprised to be asked to do so. Typically, middle school teachers in regular education are not in contact with Mom and Dad except at grading time. Even then there is little contact, since many parents do not come to parent-teacher conferences. So to be asked to provide information on a daily basis, such as keeping a journal, may be quite new for them.

Parents may feel quite discouraged in the face of the objections posed by the teachers, but should persevere anyway, since this information is crucial to the smooth operation of the overall program. However, long narratives are not necessary each day. The key is for the teachers to complete the form at the end of the day or week so that it will not intrude on the teacher's time. Information from each class can include items that are relevant to that day or week only, with only enough information entered to satisfy a very nervous parent. The following form is just one example of information gathered each day for one student. Teachers and parents should modify this form to reflect the individual student's needs and make it more relevant to all parties involved. Forms should not take much time at all to fill out, since middle school teachers do not have extra time between classes. Additional information can be added to or deleted from this form as necessary.

Student Performance Chart

Student Name: _____ Date: _____ Teacher initials: _____

Class: _____ Did: ____well ____not well _____ %participated

Homework turned in _____yes _____no   appropriate behaviors _____yes _____no
Comments:

****

Student Name: _____ Date: _____ Teacher initials: _____

Class: _____ Did: ____well ____not well _____ %participated

Homework turned in _____yes _____no   appropriate behaviors _____yes _____no
Comments:

The teachers would probably prefer to fill out a form at the end of the week, but a weekly form often does not provide the amount of information that the parents need. Also, teachers may forget to include crucial information on a weekly sheet. So, if possible, develop a daily sheet that can be easily checked off by the teachers and sent home with the student at the end of the day. The wise IEP holder will ask the parents to return it the next day for the file folder, or obtain a copy of the form before it goes home each day. These forms can provide insight into programming issues when they are viewed over time and may help to pick up problem areas before they reach crisis stage.

C. Between Regular Education Teachers

Collaboration between regular education teachers has some naturally occurring helpers. Team meetings or grade level meetings usually occur in middle school and provide golden opportunities to share information about a particular student. Conversely, these meetings may not be viewed as times to get specific regarding one student only, and may be reserved for curriculum decisions about a particular subject, or about school issues. However, teachers may be able to carve out a few minutes to share sufficient information about the student to satisfy everyone's needs. If the student is having particular problems this will not likely be enough time to solve the problems and develop new behavioral programs. Extra meeting times may need to be scheduled for coordination and the special education teacher brought into these meetings.

Collaboration between regular education teachers usually covers points which are relevant to all teachers, such as the learning style of the student, useful academic modifications, tips on behavior contracts and programs, homework issues and links to subject material. If problems persist it will be necessary to seek assistance from the special education teacher or from the parents.

D. Between Special Education and Regular Education Teachers

The IEP holder must have regular contact with the relevant teachers in order to maintain consistency across all settings. Without it, she will be handicapped in many ways and will not have the information necessary to implement the IEP objectives or to ensure that they are carried out. Prior to the meetings, she will be faced with the very real project of getting everyone together. This can be a daunting task when working with five or six teachers' schedules. She will have to solve the problem of where to get all of the teachers together, circulate schedules and lists of concerns and attempt to streamline the meetings. Regular meetings are preferable to trying to schedule new time slots for each gathering, but regular meetings should not be so frequent as to eliminate the desire to meet. A simple meeting form such as the one outlined below can help to set up the meeting.

WHEN CAN YOU MEET?

Teacher:_____   Student:_____

_____ M	_____ 3:00	List of Concerns:
_____ T	_____ 3:15	_____
_____ W	_____ 3:30	_____
_____ Th	_____ 3:45	_____
_____ F	_____ 4:00	_____
Week of	_____ 4:15	(Return to Ms. Jones)
_____		

Collaboration meetings should be short and to the point, preferably no longer than 30 minutes. Otherwise the IEP holder may find that teachers will not attend. The meeting should be structured to include the important points first with options ready to be voted on, if necessary. This will take some prior analysis based upon the responses to her circulated note, but will save time in the long run.

Regular meetings can also be used as opportunities to teach the teachers about the disability, and to present new strategies and methods for teaching someone with autism or Asperger's Syndrome. This time is valuable to support the teachers and provide guidance for their interactions with this student. Without it, regular education teachers can feel as if they are out on a limb, as well as confused and even angry that they have a student they don't understand. The IEP holder must prevent this feeling if at all possible. The IEP holder must also let the teachers know that she is not the holder of all the answers. She will be confused at times as well, and she must work closely with the teachers, resource personnel and administration to find solutions. When they have support, regular education teachers can support the program, and can also be its strongest proponents.

E. School Administration Support

The impact of any inclusion project will be much stronger whenever the IEP holder and the teachers have the support of the administration. This includes both the principal and special education director. Some middle school principals can be tough opponents of inclusive programming because they perceive a threat to the core academics and the overall authority of the administration. Some students with High-Functioning Autism (HFA) and AS oppose this authority and balk at the regulations under which typical students must function. As stated previously, many of our students with this disability face suspension and expulsion due to misunderstandings of rules and regulations, inappropriate responses to the teachers or low coping and frustration levels in time of stress. Although they may be able to perform adequately or better in academics, their interpersonal skills will pose interesting situations, to say the least, for the principals to solve. Therefore, it is wise to include the administration in any relevant meetings, invite them to training given for the teachers, ask them to speak at faculty meetings to inform all teachers on the disability (without identifying the student), and to help develop a disability awareness program for the school. These suggestions to the principal will demonstrate the willingness of the special education department to solve all of the issues surrounding the inclusion program.

What if the teachers do not have the administration's support for their student's program? Lack of support will make it much harder—but not impossible—to implement the inclusion program. Teachers and parents will have to persevere simply because the IEP prescribes the style of program for the student. The IEP is a powerful document because it is based upon federal law (IDEA), and schools must implement what has been outlined within that document.

When an IEP fails, parents end up seeking assistance from the law. The resulting lawsuits can be unfortunate in the extreme, for much is lost when this occurs. The lines between school and home become impenetrable walls in some cases. Teachers may feel their jobs are at risk and are reluctant to "go the extra mile" for a student who clearly needs it. It is certainly worth the time and effort put into trying to solve the problems of administrative support for the inclusion program. If you must, go to the superintendent's office for a "discussion" of disability awareness in the county, ideas on how to develop such a program, suggestions for principles to begin with, etc. In other words, you may have to do an end-run around the principal to their boss or the school board. But if you have to do this, please, use every diplomatic skill that you have. Leave emotions home and talk about how the programs will help ALL students, *not just your own*. You want to be viewed as a contributor to your school system, not an hysterical detractor. You will have better luck with diplomacy than with clubs.

Once the administration is behind the program, the IEP holder should find it easier to gain the support of the teachers. They take their lead from the principal, resulting in increased efforts to solve problems and to sort out difficulties. Some principals have let the teachers know that they should get used to inclusive styles of teaching or transfer to another school. Although this is drastic and doesn't happen often, it does occur. But it may alienate the IEP holder from the teachers, losing informal networks of support or friends in the school. Finding a balance is important for all concerned.

F. Between Mom and Dad

One of the most difficult situations for a teacher is to try and satisfy the parent's requests when it is evident that Mom and Dad are not in agreement themselves. Many parents have differing viewpoints on what their particular child needs and are able to work it out between themselves. Many, however, cannot resolve the conflict and they pose various diverse opinions as to the child's needs, what therapies are necessary, who should help the student in the evening with homework, who talks to a particular teacher, who presents the "family" opinion at meetings, and any number of other subjects. All of this serves only to put the teacher between the parents, trying to sort out whom she should listen to. A harrowing situation, to say the least.

When disagreements arise between the parents, every effort should be made to sort them out _prior_ to the meeting with the teachers. It is not fair to cause stress to the teachers when parents are arguing. Teachers have enough stress already - don't add to it. If there are differing opinions that can't be worked out prior to any meeting, then the parents should calmly inform the teachers that they disagree. At that point, teachers have better options available. She can:

- offer to find supporting evidence for each side in an effort to see where researchers stand on the global issue;

- offer to pick one opinion and give it a try for one month, taking data on it to judge accuracy or efficacy before meeting again for discussion;

- offer referral names of community agencies (therapists, psychologists, psychiatrists, mental health, autism society, etc.) who might be able to help the family resolve the issue better;

- ask for a supervisor's opinion as to which direction to go.

Teachers do not like being placed between a mom and dad who are arguing about a child's program. It causes great stress, a feeling of wasted time and frustration, lengthens the time prior to a student's intervention, and adds countless hours to an already too-long meeting. Therefore, it is well worth the time spent resolving issues before going into a meeting with your child's teachers.

G. Between School and Community Therapists

Many students with autism/AS have outside therapists who help them learn new skills. These include speech therapists, occupational therapists or social skills therapists. Many students also receive extra tutoring in math and reading to assist their middle school academic achievement. Some receive this assistance during the school term or over the summer. Although parents are usually pleased that they are able to access community services for their child, often the money spent on these therapies is wasted simply because no mechanism is in place for true collaboration across settings. Our students can learn and be helped by many interventionists. However, when generalization of skills is not addressed up front, the benefits may be questionable because the child may not exhibit the skills elsewhere.

Another issue between home and school therapists is that neither knows what the other is teaching. Many times the parties have never met. Collaboration between the school speech therapist or OT and their community counterparts should occur at least once per month, even if it is just a phone call, so that ideas can be exchanged, progress noted, and the individual program streamlined for both settings. Without this type of collaborative effort, you will likely end up with a very confused child, since there is no continuity in his therapy. Our students with autism have enough to face in this confusing world; we certainly do not need to build in additional confusion and expect them to cope.

H. Between Paraprofessionals and Supervisors

Paraprofessionals are in a tough position in an inclusive setting and a good parapro is worth her weight in gold. Collaboration is tough, with different instructions constantly given from a variety of sources. The paraprofessional receives directions from both the special education teacher and the regular education teacher.

Who truly supervises the parapro? This depends upon where the funding for her position comes from. If she is considered a "classroom" paraprofessional paid through regular education funds (rare in middle school), then her boss is the regular education teacher. However, if she is placed in the setting to support a child with a disability, then her role is completely different. She is supervised through the special education teacher, *NOT* the regular education teacher. But this poses new problems. Unless this is a collaborative classroom, the parapro may never see her boss!

Establishing collaborative roles for the paraprofessional is an important first step that *must* be decided before setting up the collaborative roles between special and regular education teachers. This will make the parapro much more comfortable in her job, and give her a clearer identity. Parapros assume a great deal of responsibility for the student's behavior and academic programs, requiring on-going collaboration with the supervising teacher and with the regular education teacher in order to best support her student. The regular education teacher can direct her, but this subject should be discussed before she is assigned to the student. Neither should she become the sole teacher. Marks, Schrader, and Levine write:

> *. . . assuming sole responsibility rather than a shared one with the classroom teacher cannot be viewed as acceptable, (1999).*

Keep this in mind when addressing collaborative roles with your inclusion program. Give the parapro a break and don't expect her to take the role of the teacher. She has not been trained in that capacity.

I. Treatment Team Meetings

We have referred throughout this book to "treatment team meetings." Just what are those? And what aren't they? A treatment team meeting is simply a routinely scheduled period that has been set aside to gather all relevant staff and parents for a fast look at the program. This is _not_ an IEP or problem-solving meeting! This meeting style is only designed to help identify areas that need attention, or to ensure everyone is continuing to stay on track. Team meetings shouldn't last any longer than 20-25 minutes and some teachers set a timer to stay within these boundaries. Admittedly, once everyone comes together you may find the meetings go longer, but that is then up to the people involved. Try to keep the meetings short and sweet, and you will have a better likelihood of any involved staff showing up. Don't assume that everyone involved with this student will show up every time. It doesn't happen. But they should all be invited and made to feel welcome.

Treatment team meetings should be scheduled about once a month, if possible. This is usually enough time to try out suggestions from the last meeting and to identify other solutions. It is also a good "bonding" time for teachers so that they feel their efforts are appreciated and respected, and that they are supported by both the IEP holder and the parents. Parents, for goodness sake, bring the brownies or cookies to the meetings. It's hard to argue with one another when you're sharing goodies brought in especially for you! Don't forget to invite the PE coach, music/band instructor, art teacher, after-school club supervisor, etc. They like to know that they are contributors, as well.

Treatment team meetings can be fun, informative, and can offer a wealth of information about a student's program. But try not to make *major* decisions based upon the 20-25 minute session. Just identify where the work needs to be done, then make your plans with only those relevant staff. The IEP holder may learn that she needs to meet only with the math teacher to sort out a particular modification; or she may have to provide the science teacher with articles on peer tutor programs. She may also learn that she needs to attend the after-school club because something is going wrong and the supervisor hasn't a clue how to handle it.

A Note to Special Education Teachers

Collaboration takes work, but it doesn't have to be unpleasant or time consuming. The IEP holder assumes much of the responsibility for this area, as she does for all of the education of a student with special needs. Are we piling too much onto her plate? Unfortunately, yes we are. That's why the special education teacher needs to be organized and trained and well supported by *everyone and on every side*. Without that encompassing support, she may be in deep trouble and leave the profession quickly. There is a huge shortage of special education teachers in today's society. Let us find all avenues to stop this from happening and retain the good teachers. This author is quite certain that many teachers will read the material in this section and go screaming into the night because of all the meetings. That is certainly not the intention! You need help and assistance – learn where to seek it, how to get it, and then share the knowledge with everyone. Our society is better off because you are in the trenches with us, improving human lives for all.

9

Other Programming Issues to Consider

A. Teacher Exhaustion or "Burnout"

Teacher exhaustion, or "burnout", is a large concern of both school and home environments. This is especially true when the teacher is working with an intensive program such as those for students with autism/AS. Such programs tend to be time-intensive and require on-going analysis and monitoring from a number of people, making it easy for those involved to become exhausted, less receptive to new ideas and solutions, and sometimes tired of the very subject of "autism." Factors that can cause teacher burn-out include:

1. _Behavior Programming:_ Regular education teachers who are unfamiliar with the amount of programming necessary to support appropriate behaviors with students with autism/AS can become frustrated and overwhelmed in the face of the daily data collection, functional analysis of behavior process, motivational surveys, and constant fine-tuning of the program. In addition, teachers better accept reactive plans and response cost plans because they typically only have to pay attention to the student's inappropriate behaviors. Positive systems take much more attention, causing teachers to feel frustrated when they have missed opportunities to reinforce the better, more appropriate behaviors.

2. _Student Behavior Outbursts:_ Outburst behaviors, which can include screaming, crying, yelling, throwing materials, aggression and other inappropriate behaviors, can surprise and fluster many regular education teachers unfamiliar with this disorder and send them screaming into the principal's office. In fact, these behaviors can fluster special education teachers as well, especially when the behaviors prove resistant to interventions. In the face of ongoing pressure to solve these puzzles, many teachers cannot cope with the demands and may burnout. Also, if aggression means someone is hurt (and in middle school our students are often much larger and more powerful), teachers can reel from the sheer magnitude. Teachers who face this exhaustion may fall back on the "zero-tolerance" rule of the school and ask for the student to be suspended as a result of the behaviors. This has become an easy and ready answer for the behaviors, but does not provide real solutions.

3. *Lack of coordination:* For any program to run smoothly, coordination between environments and domains needs to be smooth and flawless. However, coordination of services often does not occur for numerous reasons, including too many teachers involved, no real planning time, scheduling conflicts, a new roster of teachers every grading period (for electives), lack of motivation, lack of structure to the meetings, resistance to including students with autism/AS, etc. As a result, special education teachers can become quite frustrated and upset trying to coordinate all of the middle school teachers. Regular education teachers can also become upset when they face continual demands to meet or coordinate efforts, especially if the meetings run long, or they become bogged down in minutia, and real solutions are not offered to problems presented.

4. *Paperwork:* The amount of paperwork that is now required by law for any special education student is tremendous. The SST process is also cumbersome, involving much paper shuffling between numerous teachers. An inclusive program for someone with autism/AS necessitates a high level of coordination through forms which analyze, detail, and summarize the various components of the program. Regular education teachers are not used to this large amount of paperwork for just one student and may balk at the idea of completing them. Since the special education teacher is usually the IEP holder, she also needs to be the main collector of the routine, daily information, making it a nightmare for the teacher who has underdeveloped organizational skills. It is often very easy to become out-of-compliance with the IEP if the special education teacher does not keep up with the daily information schedules. This causes frustration, anxiety over missed deadlines, and eventual burn-out.

5. *Intensity of parents:* All parents of students with autism/AS should be viewed as the true experts on their child, as well as his strongest advocates. They should be involved with the program every step of the way. Sometimes, however, the parents can be perceived as so intense, insisting on direct, on-site involvement every day, that the teachers feel as if their every move is monitored and that nothing they do is good enough.

Some teachers may be able to handle this situation very well, but others may not have the personal strength to cope with this type of involvement. This situation often ends with teachers who thoroughly enjoy teaching the student and want to teach him for many years, but who will not offer to do so because they are not capable of defining reasonable boundaries with the parents.

Parents who prowl the halls, looking for teachers to conduct impromptu meetings, pull teachers out of classes, send volumes of written materials to read, call the teacher each night to discuss programming, or leave numerous messages are sure to alienate the teacher. This may eliminate any good intentions that the parent may have had in making the contacts. In some cases, this means that the principal ends up setting boundaries for parent contact. He may even obtain a restraining order, restricting parents from school property without prior arrangements. As infuriating as this can be, some principals do not see other options to solving the situation. The principal's role is to protect the teacher so she can do her job of teaching. When such situations occur, no one is a winner. This has become an issue with some schools in the nation, which is truly unfortunate, since this means that school/home collaboration is at an end. Many times this ends up with lawyers becoming involved with the program.

6. _Legal Issues:_ When legal issues arise or lawyers become involved with students' programs, teachers worry about their jobs. At meetings, every word could be recorded, the courts can scrutinize data logs and lesson plans and teacher's training can be diminished and called into question. Teachers may leave the profession because they cannot teach with lawyers hovering over their shoulders. Courtrooms take their toll on the roster of teachers each year. Even if the teachers are found to be doing everything right and shown to be excellent teachers, the experience of going through an intensive legal proceeding can scare many of them into leaving their chosen profession. Burnout can occur quickly when the situation, whether right or wrong, has come to this point.

7. _Lack of training:_ Teachers conducting inclusive programs for students with autism/AS require on-going training. When they don't have it, teachers can become frustrated and upset. Dedicated teachers try very hard not only to do what is required, but also to go the extra mile. However, when they feel as if they are asked to do programs they don't understand or are ill-equipped to do, the teachers will feel inadequate and frustrated by a system which doesn't think enough of them to provide the support they need. When repeated requests for information, training or materials go unheeded, teachers will begin to believe they are not treated as professionals, leading to disillusionment with their administration in particular, and teaching in general.

1. How Do We Prevent Teacher Burnout?

Teacher exhaustion must be avoided. When teachers have reached this point, they are much less willing to try new ideas and suggestions and are less consistent in programming. Therefore, the parents and administration should find ways to prevent teacher burnout whenever possible. There are several levels at which this can be addressed. For example:

1. Teacher training – Although we have already talked about this in great detail, it is worth mentioning again that teacher burnout can be prevented by an administration

that is pro- active, not *reactive*. It is much easier to do up-front training so teachers are prepared and ready for the student, than to play catch-up, propping up teachers who show classic symptoms of burnout.

2. Parent Understanding – Students with autism can be difficult to teach. Placing them in special or regular education classrooms will not cure their disability, but it will allow them to learn new skills. However, in the course of this, they may show extreme behaviors. Parents should understand that a teacher's main goal for her job is to teach, but she often struggles when faced with the day-to-day aggression that we sometimes see. Parents should let teachers know that they appreciate their efforts at finding the function of the behaviors, and help them seek solutions and answers for the behavioral outbursts. After all, if the child is having the behavior problems at school, it is highly likely that the behaviors are occurring at home, too. Therefore, parents should *offer* to work closely with the teacher to find solutions. Teachers will appreciate offers to help solve the situation, rather than having to assign blame for not instantly finding these often-elusive answers.

3. Classroom support – It is difficult when student's IEPs states that they are to have particular services, such as inclusion, mainstreaming, or paraprofessional support, but the promised support is absent. This is frustrating for teachers who want to proceed with their program but are unable to because of administrative delays or snafus. Making sure that the teacher has what is necessary to carry out the IEP can go a long way to eliminating teacher burnout.

4. "Going the extra mile" solution – i.e., parents delivering a plateful of anything chocolate! Seriously (and who says chocolate isn't serious?), occasional treats for the teachers, treats which have nothing whatsoever to do with teaching, can tell the teacher that you think highly of her personally, not just professionally. Examples of other special treats, both professional and personal, can be gift certificates to school stores or local spas or classroom donations (within regulations) of furniture, computers, etc. Work with the school PTO for some of these. Other teacher reinforcers can include paid attendance at conferences of interest, books on the topic of autism/AS for the school library, offers to help plan and present disability awareness classes at school, hosting teacher appreciation lunches or formal dinners, etc. One effective method to bolster the wavering spirits of a good teacher is to send a letter of support to their supervisor. This can be placed in their permanent files, helping them to gain administrative support and possible raises in salary.

There are always ways to show teachers that you appreciate their hard work for your child or student. This can help a teacher understand that you appreciate their work and efforts to help your child learn and progress. Parents often become so worried about the future of their child and how much they are (or are not) progressing, that they lose sight of an individual teacher's efforts. Keep this in mind during the school year.

2. What to do When . . .

There may come a time when one particular teacher may be so exhausted by the efforts of teaching the student or class that they are no longer helping the child to progress and may actually be hampering the program. What do you do then? If this is your situation, then you will have to make some hard decisions regarding your student. Some options at this point can be:

- Calling a Treatment Team or an IEP meeting to address the issue. Why is the student causing such stress for the teacher? Is he not progressing academically? Behaviorally? What IEP objectives are not being met? What do the data show? Is the teacher teaching to the objectives or are they being left behind in favor of behavior management?

- Re-analyzing the behavior program. Why is the present program not working? What is the frequency of occurrence? (Go back to the behavior section in this book and start the process of functional analysis.)

- Re-analyzing the child's profile. What type of teacher does the child learn from best? Is that what they have now? How do they learn content? Are they visual or auditory? Is the teacher using the appropriate methods? What if everyone agrees that the current student-teacher match is not appropriate? Is there another regular education classroom that they can attend instead? Look at schedules to see if someone else could teach him the same subject. However, if the problem lay with the special education teacher, you may be faced with a larger problem.

- Look at other special education teachers in the middle school who may be able to support your student (resource teachers, self-contained teachers, teachers for students with Learning Disabilities, etc.).

- If there is no other special education teacher, you may be faced with a school move to place your child in a different middle school where the special education teacher is more receptive. But don't be surprised if your child is already known at the other public schools. Teachers talk among themselves and word gets out regarding "problem students," whether the student is at fault or not.

- If the situation of teacher burnout is such that your child's learning is totally compromised, then you may want to look at private schools in your area, although they may or may not be willing to accept a student with this disability. Unfortunately, the term "autism" often scares private schools and many have policies that don't allow them to accept students with this disability. Right or wrong, this goes on.

- A last option is home-schooling your child. Unfortunately we have many students who are home-schooled because of the increased level of difficulty experienced during middle school. We also have many more who are home-schooled because the level of teasing and bullying was too great. That is, indeed, unfortunate since you have then lost access to the typical students and the wide diversity of opportunities that could be experienced in the social realm. Homeschooling isn't the option for everyone, so carefully study all these options before making your decision. Should homeschooling be your solution, then make sure that there are plenty of outside social opportunities.

B. Transition to High School

Transition issues are not just for the high schooler moving into adulthood. They are for the middle school student, as well. Hughes, et al., (1997) states:

> . . . interventionists are waiting until students are out of school or almost ready to exit school before introducing transition programming efforts. This may be too late. Both the 1990 IDEA legislation and researchers (Brown; Moore, Agran, & McSweyn, 1990; Rusch, DeStefano, Chadsey-Rusch, Phelps, & Szymanski, 1992) agree that transition programming should begin before the secondary level, perhaps as soon as a student is identified with a disability.

Moving from middle school to high school can be just as scary as starting middle school, and issues of "what will this child do in adulthood" should be at the forefront of everyone's minds during this process. Much of the success of this latest transition (into high school) will depend upon prior analysis and on a concentrated effort to make sure all the bases are covered. Let us first consider the transition issues into high school and how we can help to plan for the high school years.

High school can be difficult for our students with autism/AS, but at least the typical peers have a higher level of social maturity than they do in middle school. Teasing and victimization still occur in this environment, targeting vulnerable and "shy" students. It is worth all your efforts to make sure your students coming into the high school environment are not easy targets for students who are not familiar or receptive to them. But let's start at the beginning; after all, at this time, your student is still in middle school, right?

The following items are excerpted from: Wagner, S. (2001). "Build Me a Bridge: Successful Transitions Through the Educational Years for Students with Autism/AS," Part 2. *Autism Digest*, March/April, 26-28.

In the Prior Spring:

1. In the last year of middle school, parents should ask their student's teacher to prepare a full portfolio of their child's work. Examples of academics to include are: science, math, language arts, social studies, art, and any other electives, social skills, and any written behavior plan that has been in operation during the last portion of the year. It would also be helpful to outline past behavior plans that have worked, and why they were stopped. Sometimes, past behavior plans can prove helpful when old behaviors return to cause disruptions in learning. Conduct a classroom version of student assessment, including a motivational survey (look in the Appendix for examples).

2. At this time of your child's education, you may very well be asked to choose the diploma track that your child will earn when they graduate from high school. Yes – it is much too early! – why do they need to know this now?! However, schools will ask you to do so because they will need to line up classes so that your child will earn enough credits to graduate. Although it is understandable, it is still difficult to make this kind of decision so early in the life of the student. With some children the answer will be easy – a college prep diploma. However, for others it may be very difficult. Some of our children will not be going on to college, just as some typical students do not. For them, a vocational track may be best. Students with a disability also have the option of a special education diploma or a certificate of attendance (options will vary in each of the states, of course). Parents should consider each of the options very carefully because it is often exceedingly difficult to change tracks in mid-high school if the student decides to pursue another avenue. In addition, if you foresee the chance of your student going on to college, or taking vocational or technical classes in a junior or community college, please be aware that many colleges and universities will not accept a special education diploma or the lack of a GED. So consider all avenues very carefully, prior to choosing a particular diploma track.

3. Determine if your high school has a traditional or "block" schedule. Your child's teacher should help to prepare the student by making up "mock" schedules and helping the student understand them before transitioning into this environment.

4. Consistency is just as crucial in high school as it has been in middle school. In high school, the student will have even more opportunities to be taught by even

larger numbers of teachers than in middle school. Develop a plan for coordination among teachers. Pull any forms that have been used in middle school and modify them for the high school, if necessary. Make sure that one of the high school team members is the IEP holder, and that that person understands her/his role for coordinating efforts among all teachers and the home setting.

5. Talk to the teacher about the possibility of a student mentor for your student to shadow for a few days, if necessary. This peer should be A CURRENT ninth grader who will be sympathetic and understanding of someone transitioning into high school. The teacher will need to have some time to find the student and talk to his parents.

6. Discuss social skills training at the last IEP or before. How will they receive social skills instruction? Not all schools do this training, so inquire how your student or child can have their need for social skills instruction met. Discuss both direct and incidental teaching with individuals and in small groups that have gone on through middle school. This may be very difficult if the high school does not offer these services.

7. Ask the high school if they have any formal peer tutoring or mentoring programs in which your students can enroll. Many schools do, though as the emphasis on academic performance becomes greater and the number of credits for graduation increases, the mentoring programs are often eliminated.

8. Ask the school to identify receptive eighth grade students who will be advancing to ninth with your student. One or more may be chosen as mentors and supporters of your student with autism/AS.

9. Identify behaviors which may be problematic. Conduct an updated functional analysis, or at least define targeted behaviors so the high school teachers will clearly understand the level of difficulty. This does not mean to place more importance on areas of challenge and not on areas of strength. But it is a mistake to leave the high school teachers guessing as to potential areas of difficulty, and be ignorant of precursors and methods to control aberrant behaviors. Don't make them "re-invent the wheel."

10. Start investigating person-centered planning programs. This will be a preliminary meeting to start defining long-term goals. Call a meeting with key personnel who are important to the student, including family members, therapists (both school and community), teachers, etc. Invite anyone who could possibly have input to preliminary decisions as to where this student will be as an adult. Problem-solve

and brainstorm different scenarios for the student when he leaves the high school setting and enters adult services. This will help to define areas and avenues to explore in the coming years.

11. Conduct an informal survey of high school peer's style of dress. As in middle school, peers are exceptionally sensitive to dress and appearance. Parents usually don't have a clue in this area. Pick the brains of high school teachers and even family friends who have high schoolers. Usually, clothing is the easiest area to change to make our students "fit in" with their peers, but too often, parents do not appreciate the level of importance this area commands with the typical peers. It is important that they do so.

12. After the teacher has identified a potential student, find out who has been assigned as the peer buddy for your student. It should be someone who is well known and liked by your student. If at all possible, have this student, and any others who can be tracked with your student, assigned to the same classes for the first grading period. This will alleviate some of the transition fears that can occur for upcoming freshmen.

In the summer, prior to starting high school:

1. About two or three weeks before school commences, start mimicking the school schedule by getting your child up at the appropriate time. Begin having the child do some homework during the day, have snacks and lunch the same time as they would during school. This will help him adjust to the new schedule.

2. Invite the peer buddy over to become more familiar with your child, if possible. Supervise them well, but allow them time to "hang out" together.

3. Take your child and the peer buddy to the school and walk the halls; find their lockers and their classrooms. Say "hi" to the principal, assistant principal and secretaries as well as any teachers who are there.

4. Once school starts, ask the peer buddy to meet your child at the door to help them transition for a few days.

5. Make sure that the peer buddy will sit with your child for lunch, if at all possible. Have him introduce your child to other students so that they become comfortable with the environment.

6. Set up the first Treatment Team Meeting for approximately 4 weeks into the school term. Set future meetings at that first meeting. Invite all the teachers, parents, and related staff to the meeting.

Many of the issues outlined above can help parents and teachers with decisions that need to be made regarding general transition issues. There is still a wealth of knowledge needed for the transition to adulthood, and since this is a middle school manual, we will leave the in-depth look at this area to subsequent books. However, we hope that parents will copy the above comments and use them to help conduct the long-term planning that is necessary for our students with autism/AS.

C. Middle School Mentality

Many parents and teachers of students in elementary school feel that the atmosphere in the middle school will be similar to what they have already experienced in the lower grades. This is far from the truth. Middle school atmosphere and mentality is much more "business-like." Middle school teachers feel that it is their business to stop "babying" the student and get them ready for high school and the real world. Teachers will often use what is best described as "tough love" in their methods of discipline, hoping that the child will "grow up quickly to face the rigors of high school," as one teacher explained. Teachers are less likely to be flexible in their grading of work performance, will demand that the student perform to the levels of the typical peers if they are included, and are less sympathetic of failure. This places a tremendous burden on the special education teacher to educate the regular education teachers about this disorder. She will find this to be a fairly easy task if the included student has a significant profile such as severe autism and/or cognitive impairment because it will be fairly evident that the student requires modifications and accommodations.

However, if her student has Asperger's Syndrome, this will be tougher. Students with AS are often viewed as manipulative and lazy, unmotivated and oppositional. It is often difficult for teachers to understand the underlying disability unless they make the effort to read the records, study up on the disability and begin taking part in the treatment team meetings. The special education teacher, therefore, should provide them with articles and information on autism/AS as well as student-specific information, so that they can begin to understand this confusing disability.

The "tough love" mentality of teachers _does not work with students with autism_. Tough love approaches will leave the student frustrated, confused and angry and maybe even frightened. Students with this disability require positive programming, academic modifications, social skills training and a host of other accommodations that are specific to the disability and student needs. Teachers need to understand that, just because the student "looks normal" does not mean that they do not have a disability. Difficulties in perception, processing and perspective-taking, along with differences in motivation, will make it appear that the student doesn't care, and doesn't want to care, about work performance! This may raise the teachers' eyebrows and tempers rapidly, and your student could be in serious trouble. Training and on-going technical assistance can help the teachers to understand the disability and learn to appreciate this complex child. Without it, middle school teacher mentality can quickly escalate the initial problem to unbelievable heights, endangering the inclusion program, the student's mental health and overall educational progress.

Certainly this does not mean that the student shouldn't learn the natural consequences of his actions in school. Our students do need to learn that their behaviors have an effect on the world in general, as well as on teachers and other students in particular. Therefore, natural consequences need to be a part of their behavior program, but they should be incorporated into the larger behavior program that is conducted for the student. Students with this disability should not be functioning under a response cost system (a negative-based system) as a sole method of behavior control. They require much more than the knowledge of natural consequences. Please refer back to the behavior section in this book for further discussion of this subject.

Although many middle school teachers have a set mentality about our students, not all of them do. There are many tremendous middle school teachers out there who already understand the disorder, or are willing to learn, and who welcome the challenge to their levels of expertise. Many middle school teachers welcome students with disabilities into their classroom with open arms and work closely with the special education teacher in co-taught classes to make sure that the student has high levels of success. Please do not assume that because we mention the reverse situation here that it is the standard. In fact, the standard may very well be the opposite—with warm, welcoming and understanding middle school teachers everywhere. We all hope your student will find many of them in his or her middle school. It will be up to the special education teacher to help find these wonderful teachers in the school and to work closely with them in programming for their student with autism/AS. Therefore, don't assume the worst in teachers, but expect and look for the best.

D. Dress Code

Some middle schools have policies that require students to wear uniforms daily. Dress uniforms work in favor of our students, since this eliminates the peer pressure regarding styles of clothes. But it can also cause tremendous headaches for parents trying to change their child's restrictive personal dress code. Most public schools, however, do not have uniforms and our students often look "geeky" to the typical peers because they do not pick up on the latest styles of clothing, hair or accessories. Parents try their best to keep their student's style of dress similar to the typical peers so that they are not providing opportunities to be teased or bullied, but parents frequently do not know what is in style. One year the typical students are all wearing a particular brand of shoes, sweatpants and cool socks. The next, sweatpants are no longer seen anywhere and only denim jeans with the crotch at the knees and sloppy shirts are seen in schools. It is difficult for parents to keep up with trends, but it is important that they do so. Our students with autism/AS are particularly vulnerable to teasing from a number of sources that are difficult to control; clothing shouldn't be one of them. At least this is one area that can be under control of the parents and teachers, but it will take coordination between the two to keep up with styles. If at all possible, teachers should inform the parents of the current fad among the typical peers so that they can acquire the appropriate styles.

Of course, this won't be possible for many parents, and teachers need to be sensitive about this issue. There is no need to humiliate parents who cannot afford to keep their students outfitted in the latest styles. Other measures can be discussed, such as making sure that, even if not outfitted in the latest style, the student is at least clean and well groomed. Clean hair is a must. Although students parade around with simple to outlandish hairstyles, the hair is generally clean. Nothing turns a peer off more at this age than greasy, filthy hair or body odor. Since our students with autism/AS usually don't care about their hair or body, parents and teachers must lend some guidance in this area to make sure that the student is clean, and that he wears deodorant at the very least. Body hormones are changing at this time of life, requiring extra efforts to eliminate any unpleasant smells, which may turn away potential friends.

As long as we are talking about dress codes, let's wander into the subject of "dressing out" for P.E. This can be a very sensitive issue for our students in the middle school.

Middle school coaches often require their students in P.E. to dress out for the sports activities. This can be a rough time for typical students who have become conscious about their own body image and how they compare physically to someone else. It's a time of pride and embarrassment, of teasing and of being teased. Students with autism/AS usually do not do well in this situation. If the coach insists on the student dressing out, he may very well find that the student with autism/AS skips gym class, becomes angry or outright refuses (though of course, there are always exceptions).

This situation seems to be more common among students with Asperger's Syndrome than students who have a more classic profile of autism, since students with AS are often more aware of "fitting in" with their peers. Either way, it is important to pay attention to this situation and try to predict the student's reactions. Alternatives can be offered to this student, such as wearing their street clothes (as long as they change their shoes), changing into gym clothes in the coach's bathroom, coming early to change clothes, etc.

Alternatives to dressing out should be found because this situation can set the tone of the student's participation in the activities. Students with autism/AS already have enough to face in the highly competitive world of the locker and sports arena. Don't make it worse by embarrassing or shaming them into dressing out when in the long run, the student can still perform the activity in non-gym type clothes. *A note of caution is necessary, however*: parents and teachers should realize that if the student wears street clothes instead of the required gym clothes, they may be teased by their peers. Coaches must be aware that this can occur and can prevent the situation by gathering up sympathetic peers who can help to shield the student from teasing, or offer higher levels of supervision.

E. Lockers

In middle school, students may now be assigned an individual locker to house their personal belongings, including books, papers, coats, backpacks and everything that adolescents carry on a daily basis. In elementary school, students usually had areas in their classrooms to place their belongings, and some have lockers in the upper grades.

Lockers are supposed to be kept neat and tidy, though at this age, few are. Because some students use lockers as storage space for items which may violate school rules, some middle schools have done away with them. But not all, obviously.

One of the reasons that we see difficulties with students with autism/AS in middle school is due to these very same lockers. The noise coming from the crashing locker doors in the hallways and in the locker rooms of the gymnasiums can be quite disturbing to our students. The noise level is quite high when 100-200 students are all opening and closing the doors of their lockers at the same time. To this noise, add the noise of 100-200 students all talking at once (because this is one of the few times they can talk), and you have noise levels that can be intolerable to our students.

How can included students avoid this situation and still be able to tolerate middle school environments? Teachers may have to investigate several ways to eliminate the noise levels for their individual students. This may include wearing soft ear plugs just prior to transitions, or dismissal two or three minutes prior to the bell so that they can get to their locker and to the next class before all the students get into the hallways. Perhaps they can even go directly to their next class without going to the lockers at all because their books are kept in the appropriate classroom. This can help the student avoid high-intensity noise.

Some teachers try to conduct desensitization programs with the student, so that the student is rewarded for tolerating longer periods at high noise levels. However, some teachers have seen limited success with this method, since sensitivity to noise levels does not appear to be a voluntary action, but rather a sensory one. Some students with autism/ AS who have come from very loud, chaotic elementary school classrooms may have an easier time tolerating the middle school noise level. This is not always certain and is not predictable. Expect to discuss this subject with the student's teachers, parents and the administration.

F. Changing Classes

By the time the student has entered middle school he has usually adjusted, somewhat, to the change of classes and teachers, since most fifth grade teams try to introduce this pattern in the elementary school years.

Middle school is more intensive and students should expect to change classes every grading period (every 9 weeks) or at least every semester, depending upon electives. This changing of classes is tough on typical students but can be horrendous for students with autism/AS. Because we continue to be presented with difficulties in transitions and changes with this disability, the student's IEP holder will need to prepare the student for these changes and help them to get adjusted to following a schedule. Some tips for the special education teacher and parents include:

- Working with the registrar or main office the previous spring to choose classes that will meet the student's needs. Students with autism/AS shouldn't be faced with their toughest classes the first grading period, if there is a choice. For example, leave P.E. until a later grading period. However, this may not be possible – the teacher may have to assign the classes as a matter of policy and regulations.

- Parents should be given the student's schedule prior to the beginning of the year so that they can help to prepare their child ahead of time.

- Prior to school starting, the student should go through the entire school day on a mock schedule. The parents can walk their child through the empty classrooms, mimicking a day's schedule, using shorter time blocks to do this.

- Also by the time school starts, the student should have already met his teachers for each of the classes. This will help him remember the roster of teachers and where their classrooms are located in the school.

- Develop an individual class list for the student to carry with him each day. The list should show the class subject, teacher's name and room number. He may not need this list for long, but he should have it at the beginning of school, and a new one every time the student's class roster changes. This list will provide a level of comfort for the student and help with lowering anxiety levels about where he needs to be at particular times.

Changing classes does not have to be traumatic for our students. Once learned, our students usually do very well with this area. But prior preparation will be necessary and should not be forgotten in the rush to start school in the fall, or when every new grading period starts.

G. Working in Groups

The very nature of this disability means that students with autism/AS usually prefer to work in isolation, rather than in groups. In middle school they will be provided with many opportunities to do so through daily and weekly assignments. However, they will also be called upon to work in small groups more frequently than they did in elementary school, usually on class assignments or projects. Our students are more or less successful with these assignments, depending on the level of severity of their disability, and their interest in the subject material. For the most part, students with autism/AS can contribute a wealth of information on favored topics, but when it is a topic that holds no interest the student may resist. Many of our students like to take the lead and direct the project, much to the chagrin of other students in the group who do not wish to follow them as leader or who want the group to go in a different direction. The teacher may need to step in and assign roles to the students in the group, thereby settling the dispute.

Many small groups that include a student with this disability find that the other members work closely together, and allow the student with autism/AS to perform one aspect of the project alone. This ends up working well for the group, and for the student with autism/ AS, though it may not meet exact definitions of "working in a group." Students with Asperger's Syndrome may be better equipped to work within the group than someone with a more pronounced profile, but this is not a given. They may still require direction in how to share information, how to assimilate other members materials into their own, and how to perform the give and take reciprocal actions necessary to making the group work together in a cohesive manner.

Our students with autism/AS can learn to work on projects in small groups within the class structure, but the teacher may find that she must identify and explain the various steps of working in a group to the student, so that the group can produce the desired outcome. Steps to consider are:

- assigning roles within the group (leader, researcher, etc.);
- gathering preliminary opinions of the main topic;
- discussing the topic at large;
- dividing the topic into components;
- assigning components to members;
- researching individual components by the members;
- sharing each member's preliminary findings within the group;
- posing problems and solutions found with the findings;
- relating findings from one component to the other components;
- writing preliminary drafts of individual components;
- incorporating all preliminary drafts into a preliminary "sloppy copy";
- critiquing the "sloppy copy";
- writing the final draft.

Teachers usually have their own methods of explaining group projects and activities to their students and can add numerous other steps to the process. But teachers who have students with autism/AS in their class must understand that group projects will be difficult for our students, and that they will require concrete directions on performing this type of activity. Do not force the student to be ostracized by the peers or frustrated because they lack the ability to understand vague directions to "work in a group." Our students can contribute a vast knowledge of topics if they are shown how to do so. Remember, students with autism/AS usually want very much to perform to the teacher's expectations, but run into difficulties when the instructions are minimal or unclear. It is often helpful to write out the process for our students, outlining what their own roles are, what they are to do within the group, and how group projects work to completion.

H. Budding Sexuality and Raging Hormones

Middle school students are a developing, raging bundle of budding sexuality and our students with autism/AS are no different than typical students in this matter. They face the same changes in hormone levels, same changes in voice depth and the same changes in their bodies. The main difference between students with this disability and typical students is that our students don't fully understand what is happening to their bodies and do not understand the societal controls that are necessary when hormones are directing emotional reactions.

At this time of life, typical students are noticing each other more, are starting to "size each other up" and are extremely judgmental of each other's actions, as well as of their own. Emotions run high at this time and fluctuate from one end of the spectrum to the other, forcing students to react quickly to events that they might not otherwise react to with additional processing. Social status is also determined at this age, which will cause students to jockey for position in the societal hierarchy. Unfortunately, jockeying for position usually means that they must bump others to a lower level – frequently through teasing and/or bullying. Much of this can be attributed to hormones, and unfortunately our students with autism/AS do not understand any of this.

Students with autism/AS also go through this same physiological and emotional change, but to their detriment, do not understand how to engage skills that can better equip them to handle the daily situations that are posed.

The typical student's coping skills aren't that great either, but they are usually much better than our students with this disability. Students with autism/AS do not understand the physical urges that naturally occur, and how these must be kept from other people. It is not uncommon for our students to publicly grab parts of their body when they have a need to, and then not be aware or understand when other students stare or make comments about them. As a result, our students with this disability will need _specific instruction_ as to what they can and can't do in public.

Remember, our students are exceptionally concrete thinkers. They will need a parent or teacher to spell out what is expected in public and what is not. For example, the student should be told, "you may not touch your crotch in school unless you are in a locked bathroom stall." This may seem humorous to people who naturally understand this social rule, but students with autism/AS do not always understand. Delineate all the possible rules that apply to your student, depending upon their personal level of understanding.

Another area that must be discussed at this age is the sex education classes that middle school students are subjected to (with good reason, we might add). Students are provided with classes that outline sexually-transmitted diseases, abstinence, contraceptives, etc., depending upon the regulations of the state's department of education. This is a class that can totally confuse our students - often because the teacher does not present the information concretely enough to fully understand. Middle schoolers who are typically developing are really already quite sophisticated in the areas of sexuality, gathering much information from television and videogames, so teachers do not often have to cover the basic facts of sexual intercourse and the ramifications of the act. You would think that in a class that covers the basics, students would be presented with the basics, but sometimes they are not. The terms may be used, but they may not be defined. This is where our students with autism/AS run into trouble.

For example, one middle school girl with AS became very upset and was crying "I have a rash and am going to die! Will someone take me to the doctor?"

The typical students in class were, of course, smirking because they had just been shown a video about syphilis and understood how you get syphilis. This young girl did not, and assumed that because she had a minor rash on her hand, she had syphilis and would die. It was embarrassing for the teacher to have to help this distraught young lady understand the reasons why she did *not* have syphilis and that she really didn't have to worry!

How can parents help their student better understand this course work? First, they must decide if their child has the capability of understanding the entire content, or if they will have to provide different instruction in this area. They should discuss this issue with the regular education teacher, get a course syllabus, modify instructional content and format, and perhaps, teach the subject differently than is presented for the typical students. They may want to consider teaching this course away from typical students so that concrete information can be presented without the fear of sounding redundant to the other students, or embarrassing the student. They may decide to turn the whole sticky subject over to the parent to teach.

How can the content be restructured for better understanding? Teachers and parents may want to consider setting <u>concrete and specific</u> rules on how to handle potential behaviors from other people. For example, setting concrete rules for compromising situations:

1. Never getting into a car with a stranger
2. Never take off their clothes for any stranger except a doctor
3. Telling parents if someone asks to touch their private areas of their body, etc.

The best protection for someone with autism/AS is to have set routines to follow for potential situations.

Knowledge of normal body changes is a must as well. Girls at this age will need to be told of menstruation and how this is a private matter, not to be discussed with other students - *anywhere*. Of course, some girls are already experiencing their periods by this time, but certainly not all. Emergency procedures should be defined and the young girl told to whom she should go when she requires assistance. The parents and teachers (usually special education teachers at this point), should make the student clearly understand that asking the teacher for assistance should be saved for the end of class, after the bell rings. She may write the teacher a note which can be handed to her, without saying anything. She may also have a nonverbal signal to the teacher which indicates that she needs to use the restroom immediately, and requires assistance. This is much better than announcing to the class, "Teacher, I think I have started my period. May I go to the bathroom?" That will destroy any hope of friendship with the other students and usually dissolve the class into hysterics. Both special and regular education teachers need to use much sensitivity when working with this subject with our students, and realize that they may not understand that this is a private matter.

Some of our students also need to be told directly that what other subjects should not be discussed in class. When one young student with AS was asked why he was looking so puzzled, he stated, "Well, it could be because I didn't get much sleep last night, or it could be because I'm constipated." You can imagine what happened next in his classroom! By reviewing these subjects with the students, we can try to prevent these situations. They can also learn the subjects best kept to themselves.

I. Fine and Gross Motor Challenges

Fine motor challenges:

Students with autism/AS can experience motor challenges which affect their school performance. Middle school academics are really quite tough, and the expectations are that they will produce a large amount of written work in the form of reports, tests, summaries of material, problem analysis and projects. Fine motor problems will make this difficult for our students. Since they are included in regular education classes, the student will likely try very hard to comply with these expectations. Because they will fall short, you will see anxiety levels rise and motivation for school work plummet. Students with Asperger's in particular find keeping up with the work production exceedingly difficult and may very well shut down, refusing to produce any work at all. It then becomes difficult for the teacher to understand why such a bright student can not comply with the written work assignments. After all he has an I.Q. of 130, right? Parents will find teachers losing patience and beginning to punish the student through lower grades, thereby frustrating the student even more. Academic modifications are necessary for the student who faces fine motor challenges.

It is easier to recognize the need for output modifications for students who have more significant disability profiles than it is for someone with an Asperger's profile. Nevertheless, students with AS need modifications in written production as much as students with a more severe form of autism. Teachers must keep this in mind and look for ways to modify the curriculum so that they have proof the student has mastered the content or subject material.

Look to the computer for many of our students. Using hindsight, teachers and parents should have introduced keyboarding skills early, such as in elementary school, rather than waiting for a single elective in middle school. There isn't sufficient time for the student to become proficient at typing and use it for the written portions of their middle school classes. By this time, our students need to be very competent at typing; therefore, don't wait until middle school to introduce keyboarding and composition on computers. If your student has not had keyboarding previously, then pick up this class immediately upon entering middle school as it is better not to wait any longer on such a valuable skill.

Gross motor challenges:

Some students with autism have highly developed gross motor skills and can perform to typical student standards in gym classes with appropriate supports in the method of instruction. Students with AS, however, usually demonstrate significant challenges in this area; this is a part of the core disability. They will exhibit a real lack of coordination with their gait and general movement around the school, and perform much below typical student levels. Typical middle schoolers by this time are usually physically gifted. This has proven to be a very difficult situation for our students with autism/AS who cannot compete well in team or individual sports, making them the last to be chosen for any P.E. activity. Coaches should make sure that everyone in our student's classes understands that everyone performs to different levels, and that everyone can contribute in different ways. This may take some lecturing to the entire class so that they do not target the student with autism/AS for punishment because they can't keep up, or because they do not perform to the expected levels. In addition, it will be important to select a few sympathetic peers to offer additional support, and assign them as peer buddies for the student to assist them whenever possible. This must be conducted in a sensitive manner, without calling undue attention to the student's lack of ability in front of the whole class. Our students with autism/AS can enjoy P.E. when they form a close bond with the coach and a few peers, and not see themselves as failures, but as contributing members of the class.

J. Sensory Issues

Many of our students receive therapy from occupational therapists who address the sensory issues specifically as many students with autism and AS have sensory needs different from the typical students. They may require the student to perform a variety of routines or activities which will help them to desensitize themselves in the presence of sensory stimuli, or when they have become overloaded. Exact routines and activities will be outlined in the IEP after discussion by the team.

In a middle school inclusion program, it will be more difficult to imbed these activities into the regular education curriculum because they will make the student appear different from their classmates, and offer potential areas for teasing. Teachers and parents who wish to address sensory integration topics should be careful to schedule these activities or supports at times or in areas when they will not receive undue scrutiny by the typical peer. Another area of caution regarding sensory issues is that the activities used in these routines are often used as a behavior change agent. Pairing the activity of jumping with times of upset behavior may backfire, and the student may increase his maladaptive behaviors in order to gain the pleasurable activity. This scenario sends the wrong message and may create more behavior outbursts.

Nevertheless, it is important to recognize that our students get overwhelmed at times with the regular education setting and need to calm down in a safe place, such as a home-base. But conditions must be defined with a full behavior plan which can regulate the use of this strategy so that it achieves its purpose and is not circumventing maladaptive behaviors.

10

Let's Get To Know Some Middle School Kids

In this chapter, let's look at some middle school students, their schedules and their programs. These profiles are based on real students, but the names and other details have been changed to maintain confidentiality. Having said that, perhaps your student or child will resemble one portrayed here. You will be able to tell that not all students start from the same point, nor experience success at the same rate.

Obviously, modifications are made to reflect individual needs. But consider the following examples of middle school programs that facilitate both full and partial access to typical students.

Meet Charlie - Charlie is a fifth grade student with Asperger's Syndrome who is getting ready to transition to middle school. Charlie has been in regular education classes for K-5. Although his academics are fine, his social skills still lag significantly and Charlie has not developed any close friends. Charlie isolates himself and perseverates on his favorite topic, computers. However, he can be easily redirected by a teacher. Charlie is more of an introvert than extrovert. On the WISC-III, Charlie falls in the high-average range, though he has a 19-point difference between verbal and performance scores. He is very verbal, loves computers, math and art, and hates language arts and music. His handwriting is legible, but messy. Charlie doesn't like P.E. because his gross motor skills are quite delayed, giving him an uncoordinated gait and a lack of ability in team sports. He is never chosen by peers to be on their team (usually the P.E. coach assigns him to a group). Socially, Charlie is delayed, though he attempts to interact with other students and wants friends. He is eager to please but very vulnerable to peers, and has been teased, sometimes daily, by the peers. He is looking forward to middle school, though, and can't wait to learn more about computers and technology.

<u>*Transition Plan:*</u> Prior to the end of the school term, Charlie's teacher, Ms. Lomas, fills out a portfolio form (found in Appendix). She also takes the following steps:

1. Contacts the middle school resource teacher (Ms. Womack) and invites her to the IEP on May 15th at 3:00 p.m. Asks her to come and discuss Charlie on May 10th, prior to the IEP. Unfortunately, Ms. Womack will not be able to do this because of her own roster of IEP's for middle school students. She will, however, attend the May 15th meeting.

2. Ms. Lomas talks to Ms. Womack by phone prior to the IEP. She discusses school visits for Charlie and her other students.

3. Sets date to visit middle school.

4. Contacts Charlie's parents to set up a transition meeting (non-IEP Treatment Team meeting) on May 5th.

5. At May 5th meeting, discusses middle school with the parents. Discusses the upcoming visit and suggests that the parents take him to the school additional times before the end of the school term and during the summer months to maintain familiarity.

6. May 10th, all students visit Ms. Womack. Ms. Lomas had asked for Ms. Womack to select peer buddies who can help conduct the tour of the middle school for the students. Ms. Womack asks her current peer tutors to act as guides for the tour.

7. May 15th IEP. Discussed class schedule for Charlie. He will be with regular education classes for math, science, health, social studies and band. He will take Language Arts with the Resource Teacher. A tentative schedule is suggested, though this will be determined by the middle school administration. Ms. Lomas will work with them prior to the end of the school term. The first visit to the school is set for May 28th. Parents will set additional dates later.

8. Charlie's behavior program is explained to Ms. Womack. Consistency across all teachers is stressed. Portfolio information is transferred to Ms. Womack.

9. Charlie visits the middle school one more time with his mother and is escorted by a peer tutor.

10. Charlie's teacher arranges the fall plan for the transition into middle school.

11. End of school term.

Summer Plan: During the summer break, Charlie's parents take him to visit the middle school twice to meet his new teachers, once in early July and again during pre-planning, July 30th. During pre-planning, Charlie's IEP case manager (IEP holder), Ms. Womack, notifies all of his teachers of his IEP objectives and arranges to meet with them during pre-planning to provide information on the disability, and on Charlie. Of course it can't be a long meeting, since all teachers have so much to do during pre-planning.

Beginning of School:

1. Charlie arrives at school the first day (early) and is met by his new homeroom teacher, Ms. Womack. She takes him to the homeroom and introduces him to his peer buddy who will accompany him to each of his classes (See Welcome Club below).

2. Charlie meets each teacher on his IEP Team as he follows his schedule with the buddy.

3. Charlie continues on with his course work for the first nine weeks.

4. After two weeks, Ms. Womack arranges for an early morning club that Charlie can participate in before the first class bell. The students are hand-picked by the teachers in Charlie's team as being socially mature. She also selects members from the school chess club and asks that they participate as well.

5. Ms. Womack arranges for a meeting for all club members and discusses both behavioral and social rules for the club. She sets up meetings at two-week intervals.

6. Ms. Womack sets the first Treatment Team Meeting with all the teachers for one month into the term, but connects with all of them each week.

Charlie's schedule consists of the following:

Period	Class	Teacher	Room #
1st	Band	Butler	MUS103
2nd	Health	Swanson	209
3rd	Science	Tuttle	210
Lunch	——	——	***M, W 213
4th	Pre-Algebra	Czinski	213
5th	Social Studies	Lester	202
6th	Language Arts	Womack	208

Charlie does not require paraprofessional support. Since he requires social skills training, Ms. Womack has signed him up for a twice-a-week session with the school counselor. Charlie will take a sack lunch to Ms. Sargent's office to participate in a social skills session with a small group of students. (This group started up 5 weeks into the first grading period.) Ms. Sargent took the social skills assessment that was provided as part of his portfolio and used this to pull objectives for Charlie and others in the group. She will also notify each teacher of the lessons being worked on so that they may help him to generalize his skills.

Previously, Charlie's teacher also enrolled him and his classmates in the school's Welcome Club. This is an organization that helps students adjust to their new school. Duties of the Welcome Club may include greeting the student, taking them on a tour of the building, escorting them around their first day of school, offering explanations of the various programs offered. They may also introduce them to their teachers, and generally be a "friend" of the new student for the first two weeks. Club members report to the school counselor any problems that the student may be having.

Ms. Womack, the IEP case manager, tracks Charlie's behavior program. Charlie's behavior form includes targeted behaviors listed below and Charlie carries it to each class. Each teacher signs the form at the end of class. Charlie takes it to his last teacher of the day, Ms. Womack, who transfers the data to a graph. Ms. Womack is working in collaboration with Charlie's mom, and when Charlie has earned 500 points, he gets to go to a movie with his older brother without the parents along.

His form looks like this:

Period	Class	# Pt's earned	Teacher's signature
1st			
2nd			
3rd			
Lunch			
4th			
5th			
6th			

Points earned: 1 point each: Total poss: 3pts for each class. 1. Following directions 2. Using appropriate language 3. Completing assignments	Points fined for: 1. Disruptive behavior 2. Not turning in homework 3. Inappropriate language

Cash in points for _____:

18-21	Pts: 15	minutes computer at end of day.
15-17	Pts: 10	minutes computer at end of day.
13-14	Pts: 5	minutes computer at end of day.
0-12	Pts: Quiet reading time.	

Social Skills: Charlie's teachers conducted a social skills assessment which found he required intervention in the following areas:

- making and keeping friends
- staying on topic
- understanding when the listener is tired of a topic
- recognizing facial expressions
- building on topics
- using appropriate eye contact
- using non-dramatic gestures coordinated with speech
- using appropriate vocal tone

Because Charlie has several needs in the pragmatic language area, Ms. Womack approached Charlie's speech therapist to arrange for a small group speech session using three typical peers prior to the start of the day, on Tuesday, Wednesday and Thursday. This session will concentrate on conversational speech, and will target Charlie's areas of difficulty, as well as helping him to better know some of his fellow middle schoolers. At this point, eighth grade students will be selected because of their higher maturity levels.

Charlie will also join the computer club that is being organized by Ms. Womack. It will be open to any student in the school and will be held in the technology lab. Ms. Womack has several students who would enjoy this club. They will meet two times per month for 45 minutes after school. It will, unfortunately, be limited to those students whose parents can pick them up after the club. Ms. Womack felt that this time frame would be feasible for her, as well, since her son goes to this school and he wants to join the club, too.

Meet Jake- Jake is a neat student. He is happy, motivated to please others, is interested in girls and loves animals (he has three dogs, a bird and a hamster). Jake wants to be a veterinarian someday. Jake is a seventh grade student in middle school who receives educational intervention in a special education Mild Intellectual Disability (MID) classroom. Jake has a dual eligibility, both autism and MID. Jake has spent all of his educational years in special education classes (self-contained EBD, then self-contained MID). His special education teacher (Ms. Powers) wants to start some inclusion classes with him since she has attended a conference and is enthusiastic about him gaining access to typical peers. Jake has some behavioral difficulties that must be solved for his inclusion classes and will need academic modifications. Although he may be a happy, easy-going guy and does not tantrum, he does not discriminate between who he can talk to and when, who he can touch and where, and when he must buckle down and work. Jake's affection for girls has gotten him into trouble in the past, by hugging and trying to kiss them. His teachers are familiar with this inappropriate behavior and have him under supervision while in proximity to girls, disabled or non-disabled. Jake's behavior plan must be reanalyzed for the new classes and all of the teachers will need training for him to be successful in his new classes. But let's start at the beginning, where his teacher did, and program for Jake.

Class selection: Jake has a gift in music, notably piano playing, and can play by ear, though he reads music poorly. He is now taking piano lessons privately and is learning to read music, though he struggles with it. Jake is considered verbal, though he speaks mostly in short phrases and simple sentences. He is able to make his wants and needs understood through verbal language that he uses on a daily basis and he spontaneously initiates language towards others, though not to the extent of typical peers. He engages somewhat in delayed echolalia (rare), though not immediate echolalia, but is much better when singing. He can sing entire songs when he is motivated, though this doesn't happen often. His mother reports that he sings along with songs on the radio and prefers country music when playing the piano.

When analyzing Jake's strengths and areas of need for including him with typical peers, Jake's teacher (Ms. Powers) approached all of the middle school teachers on the seventh grade team to learn the schedules, where she might be able to introduce Jake, and to which team he can be assigned. Ms. Powers wants to start introducing regular education classes slowly to see how he adjusts before considering other classes. She determined that Jake would be able to be assigned to one of the seventh grade teams located on the west wing of the school (special education classrooms are located on the north wing). This means that Jake will have to travel across the school, something that he should be able to do independently.

Jake is also interested in science, though his delays cause him to fall far behind his fellow classmates. He is especially interested in biological science and animal science. His teacher decided to introduce him to both music and science initially, to see how he does. Music has no co-taught classes, of course, but science does, since there are other included students in the classroom.

Behavior: Ms. Powers next tackles Jake's behavior program. He has been under the typical management system in the special education classroom, losing privileges for infractions. Jake's present targeted behaviors include:

1. Touching others inappropriately.
2. Leaving his seat.
3. Talking out in class.
4. Not finishing his work.
5. Complaining about homework.
6. Not turning in his homework.

Jake loses 3 points for every infraction, which delays his reward of getting extra computer time (another motivator).

After examination, Ms. Powers has determined that this system is reactive and more negative based than she had intended it to be. Plus, she has determined that there are too many targeted behaviors to focus on in the inclusion classrooms. Therefore, she has changed her list of targeted behaviors to read:

1. Keeping hands to yourself.
2. Follow teacher directions.
3. Raising hand to speak in class.

Now, with these positive behaviors highlighted, Jake is put on a new point system of earning points toward extra computer time at the end of the week.

Preparation: As part of the preparation for Jake's new general education classes, Ms. Powers has called a meeting with the seventh grade team to which he has been assigned. Although he will only go into two classes initially, Ms. Powers has invited the entire team, though is certain that only the two relevant teachers will come. In this meeting, Ms. Powers has distributed the following information:

1. Characteristics of autism and Mild Cognitive Impairment.
2. Jake's behavior plan with written instructions.
3. Suggestions for redirection methods and other teaching strategies.
4. Academic modifications suggested.
5. Collaboration forms between the regular education class and the special education class teacher (co-teacher).
6. Suggestions for the first Treatment Team Meeting.
7. Suggestions for peer coaching.

Peer Programs: Because Jake is going into a music class without support, Ms. Powers meets with the music teacher as well, to describe Jake's abilities, and to identify possible peers who can be "assigned" to him when he is in the class. These peers are then provided with some instructions by Ms. Powers so that they can encourage Jake to fully participate in the music class. Ms. Powers has offered to meet with these students every two weeks for 15-20 minutes to answer questions after the initial meeting.

Second semester: Because Ms. Powers only began to analyze Jake's program for inclusion after school started, and because she needed to update his IEP for the inclusion classes, Jake's inclusion was targeted for the second semester, after the holiday break. Since she had several months prior to the beginning of the program, Ms. Powers used this time to prepare Jake, explain the classes that he would go into, introduce him to his peer buddies, and help him become comfortable with the new program. Just prior to the holiday break, Jake attended both the music and science classes and participated in the holiday break. Jake thoroughly enjoyed the classes, mostly because he knew he was not expected to do any work at that time! (Holiday parties went on after final exams.) After the holiday break, Jake attended the classes daily with the assistance of the collaborative teaching model and the peer buddies. He has had some adjustment to the format of the class and needed to learn how to "buckle down" and work. He continues to struggle with this and with homework, but has claimed ownership of his new classes and his peers. Ms. Powers is positive she will be able to add additional classes to his roster.

Meet Kris- Kris is a seventh grader with a diagnosis of Asperger's Syndrome. He has high cognitive abilities and likes to call attention to himself by being the "class clown." When the other students respond to his actions, it encourages his outrageous behaviors. Kris has made the statement that "the teachers and kids like me better when I cut up," and "the teachers say I'm 'gifted' and they laugh when I joke around." None of his behaviors has been so outrageous that they have gotten him into trouble, and the teachers do enjoy *some* of his antics. But he is easily redirected when necessary. In other aspects Kris blends in well. In elementary school he was teased daily, but in middle school his language arts teacher stopped the teasing with some intensive training of peers through awareness training of all disability and peer reinforcement classes – both social and more concrete. Most of the students in Kris's homeroom and regular classes have known him since elementary school and are aware that he has Asperger's Syndrome. They view him as "weird, but brilliant." The peers have grown up with Kris and like him, understanding that he is "different." Although they may like and understand him, Kris has only one close friend, a boy who also has Asperger's Syndrome. Kris sees him in his one segment of resource per day. The other students in his class tend to protect Kris from teasing out in the halls during transition, when he may come into contact with students who do not know him. However, since he has such a long social history with most of the students, teasing has not been a large problem to date.

Kris's schedule is typical of all students: reading, science (AIM class – gifted), language arts (AIM), math, social studies, technology and health. His scheduled classes change every six weeks, with different exploratories. Lunch is between third and fourth segments. Each segment is 50 minutes long. During his resource time, Kris receives help with math, organizational skills, and social skills. His behavior plan is also reviewed at this time.

Socially, Kris continues to require intervention. As a result, peers from his classroom were asked to make sure he does not eat alone at lunch. It was set up initially as a formal plan, but has now evolved into an informal one, with many peers self-selecting Kris to sit with during the lunch period. They have been trained to help redirect Kris's "cutting up" behaviors in class and in the cafeteria, and have done fairly well with this job over time, though they occasionally require additional suggestions and recommendations from the teacher. At this point the teachers do not do frequent training, as the peers are doing very well.

Behavior Programming: Kris has been on many behavior programs over the course of his educational years, to his benefit. He has been able to shape many inappropriate behaviors to more appropriate ones through a variety of plans. His present plan consists of a signed contract between Kris and his parents and teachers. He has three behavioral goals that he must try to achieve (these goals change over time, as needed). The last set was:

- I will complete all homework and turn it in on time.
- I will not make animal noises in class.
- I will keep all four legs of my chair on the floor.

Kris carries his contract with him all day. At the end of each class, each teacher makes a "plus" or a "minus" on his chart, depending on his success. Reinforcers received at the end of the week (consultation class on Friday) were awarded depending on the percentage of points earned. Kris picks a school reinforcer (parents provide options which have been more effective than teacher-offered choices). They have included trips to McDonalds, extra video time, staying up late, and going to the movies. If Kris has a very hard day and he can't follow his rules, he is called in to see his resource teacher, where he must remain until he regains control.

Kris has just concluded a highly effective year. He went from being a very bright, yet odd child who always tried to make people laugh, to being fairly popular. He made his school proud when he represented the seventh graders in a city-wide geography bee (his real area of intense interest – leading to an almost savant skill). He only rarely has disruptive behaviors in class and is an active participant not only in his core academics, but also with his behavior plan.

Meet James - James is also a seventh grader with autism, as well as mild intellectual impairment. James is verbal but speaks at a very slow pace, enunciating each word. He does not use contractions and his entire language is described as formal and "pedantic." He is very tall for his age and stands out as being awkward and clumsy. He is a sweet person and is well liked by his classmates and teachers alike. James interacts with his peers consistently, both responding and initiating conversations (though these subjects are all school-related). He doesn't like to turn in homework and will wait until he "absolutely has to" before complying. He is in all regular education classes, though three of them are team taught by a special education teacher. This teacher also gives him a 30-minute consultation weekly to help coordinate and track progress in regular classes.

During this consultation time, the focus has been on organizational skills and making sure he completes his homework. James also receives speech and occupational therapy each week. His classes consist of language arts, reading, math, science, social studies, chorus and P.E. Each class is a standard length (50 minutes) and exploratories change at each grading period. The three team-taught classes are language arts, reading and math.

Socially, James maneuvers around the school social setting fairly well, except that he sees only his own perspective and interacts with students only when he has a need. He understands about friendships and can be taught the concrete rules of social interactions, but does not understand the sophisticated layers of this area. He believes that everyone is his friend and does not discriminate, making him vulnerable. James has had much in the way of social programming and instruction in the past and has improved, but it appears that he will always need assistance in this area.

James is immediately identified as someone who is "different" from the typical students by his demeanor, vocal tone, social awkwardness and lack of response to the social cues around him. James has never expressed an opinion regarding his own differences, but does know that he has autism. When younger, he would say, "I can't do that – I'm autistic," but dropped this statement when he saw that his teachers wouldn't allow the easy excuse. At the present, James takes each moment as it is presented, and handles them to the best of his ability. He is usually very happy. He only becomes upset when he is asked to process information quickly, respond rapidly or comply with confusing directions. In elementary school, James would become very upset over these conditions, yell, throw materials and cry. However, he has been taught strategies which help him cope in these difficult situations. For example, he usually states, "I'm confused. Please tell me again." Or, "I can't handle this right now." This has served him well and has helped others to see that he requires more information. He still uses these phrases when he wants to delay his work, too, though not often.

James has no formal behavior plan. During his consultation time, his agenda is checked for accuracy and he is verbally praised for completing his work. He receives a soft drink for turning in his homework on time, though this is on an informal basis, only. James has had a successful seventh grade year and his eighth should prove to be very similar.

Meet Chase - Chase is an eighth grade student with Asperger's Syndrome. His Asperger's profile is quite severe. Chase also has very high anxiety levels, and an associated obsessive-compulsive disorder (OCD). In the elementary school years, Chase was in regular education classes, surviving well some days, and some days not.

By the end of elementary school, Chase could not tolerate the rapid changes that occurred in the general education classes and ended up fully self-contained in a Behavior Disorders classroom. His parents were not happy with this placement at all. Although Chase was under a very strict behavior program in this class, he was also observing students with significant acting out behaviors, and unfortunately, learning to mimic those students as well. At the start of middle school, Chase was transferred to a self-contained classroom for students with learning disabilities and remained there for all of his sixth and seventh grade years. A paraprofessional was also placed in this classroom, though the school system did not dictate that she was for Chase alone. He was not considered for placement in regular education classes because of his severe behaviors which occurred daily.

Chase was extremely rule-bound, had many obsessions which dictated his performance, and was socially distant from the other students. Examples of his obsessions:

- not touching doorknobs unless he could do it through his shirt;
- washing his hands all the time;
- ordering his books in a certain way under his desk;
- not using a pencil again if it fell on the floor;
- becoming extremely upset (and sometimes aggressive) if anyone said the word "jerk" in his presence;
- refusing to do any written assignments, and frustrating teachers trying to evaluate his work.

Chase needed to be supervised whenever transitioning in the hallways, since the typical students quickly learned about the word "jerk," and would say it in front of him. Chase was suspended for three days in his sixth grade year because he hit a student when this occurred.

Chase's sixth grade teachers had a meeting regarding his behaviors and developed a very strict, formal program, which included both a positive system and a response cost measure. This helped to improve his behaviors somewhat, though the level of his inappropriate behaviors remained high enough that his teachers worried about mainstreaming him. Medications had also been discussed with his parents, but they did not wish to place him on meds. They preferred to try food supplements and herbal remedies first. They agreed to discuss it with the family physician if there were no results from the herbal medicines.

Once Chase began taking herbal medicines, the parents and teachers tracked his levels of OCD symptoms and anxiety levels several times per day for three months. (See form in the Appendix; the parents requested the length of time.) Once the three-month interval was completed, all teachers and parents met again to review the data, both at home and at school. It was fairly obvious to all in the meeting that the herbal remedies were not making any discernible difference in Chase's behaviors. Chase's parents decided that they would take the data to their family physician to gain a medical opinion. Chase was subsequently placed on medication. The first series did not prove beneficial. The second medication, however, had a positive effect on Chase's obsessive behaviors, overall mood and tolerance levels. As a result, Chase has finished out his eighth grade year, and is looking forward to a more positive ninth grade high school experience. His transition plan includes two inclusion classes at the beginning of the school year to see how he adjusts to it, with the hopes of increasing this number over the course of his ninth grade year. His special education teacher is very hopeful that Chase will have a solid program in high school which will include much access to typical students, even though his middle school years were not very successful.

Meet Jason - Jason is a sixth grade student with a clear diagnosis of autism who is starting middle school in the fall. He has come out of a solid inclusion program for all of his elementary school years. Jason is considered a high functioning student with autism. At kindergarten age, he had the classic profile of this disability – delayed language (entered kindergarten with minimal language – just some immediate and delayed echolalia), non-existent reciprocal play skills, self-stim behaviors and very few pre-academic skills.

His mother insisted that he be placed in a regular education kindergarten classroom with a paraprofessional, even though the school system had never before conducted this style of programming. However, they did place him in a kindergarten class with a partial aide and Jason remained in an inclusive classroom throughout K-5. He had some resource assistance in the early years, but none as he entered fifth grade. Jason's cognitive functioning improved over time, and he now falls within the average range with a higher level in reading and science.

Behavior Programming: Jason requires a behavior program which helps to keep him on task. He had numerous programs in the past, which helped him, but in the fifth grade he was taught to self-monitor and to self-rate his own on-task behaviors. At the end of every 15-minute period, Jason rated himself on a scale of 1-2 (1 = off-task; 2 = on-task). At this same time his paraprofessional rated his engagement. If the two scores agreed, the parapro awarded him 1 point. If they did not agree, he did not earn a point. These ratings were conducted during academic times that required his full attention. At the end of the day, points were tallied and he was rewarded with computer time. The data on his progress show that Jason's engagement to task has increased significantly. It is this program that has helped to lay the foundation for increased attention to the lesson in middle school.

Transition Plan: Jason's transition plan was started two months prior to the end of the fifth grade school term. Jason accompanied an inclusion facilitator to the school to sit in on a few classes. He then met his potential teachers for the fall, and talked with them regarding coursework. Jason was very nervous and needed to leave the classroom to go into the hallway. It was determined that Jason would need to have a home-base during the first semester of sixth grade to help him adjust to the large environment. Jason is sensitive to loud noise, so he will transition to the next class one minute prior to the bell. The inclusion facilitator and the principal of his elementary school will select several students for tracking with Jason's classes next year. Also, the inclusion facilitator will invite his new teachers to the IEP, and to a special workshop to be held during pre-planning for all teaching staff receiving students with autism. This will help ensure that he has several familiar students in each of his classes who can help him if needed. Jason's teachers are quite optimistic regarding his next year.

Meet John - John is another high-functioning student with autism. He has a moderate profile of this disorder and exhibits many outbursts of behavior. He has been tried in the mainstream classes over the course of his elementary school years, but was based in a classroom for students with behavior disorders and then in classrooms during his learning disabled years in the lower grades. Too often in the past John was sent into his mainstream classes because his teachers felt he could do the work, but without any preparation or assistance from a paraprofessional or aide. As a result, he would have frequent loud meltdowns, meaning that he was immediately sent back to his special education classroom where he would be placed in time out, usually for 5-10 minutes. John's parents were still in favor of putting him in the mainstream classes, though John hated them. He ended up his fifth grade year very upset and frustrated over his entire program. It was decided at that time to have his IEP in the spring, prior to the start of his sixth grade year, to discuss and plan for the middle school environment.

In this meeting, John's self-contained resource teacher was again presented with his parents' suggestion that he receive exposure in some way to typical peers. This was requested even though they recognized that he still required some academic and behavioral assistance from

the special education teacher and that he had experienced great difficulty in the past. John's new teacher, Ms. Hart, was dubious about this plan because of his history, but decided to set up an additional meeting with the parents to explore John's history a little more, and to gain a better insight into his capabilities. After both meetings and meeting John, Ms. Hart felt that John's exposure to the typical students was poorly conducted and that the difficulties were not all his fault. As a result, she agreed to find ways that John could receive the input from the typical students, without causing him so much frustration and stress, or causing him to melt down. Therefore, Ms. Hart decided to begin before school and to "take it slowly," building on success. She started by inviting a few age-mates into her classroom to get to know John and her other students better. They were able to participate in various games, played computers together and just talked. The typical peers learned that John was quite bright and knew a lot about computer games. They decided that he had some "cool" qualities.

Since this session went so well, she began having a lunch club in her room for any students that wanted it. John did, and so did some of the typical peers, since they got to "hang out." After the first grading period, Ms. Hart asked the typical peers if they would like to have John accompany them to one of their classes. By this time John was quite comfortable with the peers, and they with him. The peers, John and Ms. Hart decided to have him join them in science class. Ms. Hart arranged this with the teacher, also providing her with information about John and the disability.

John now attends science class with his age-mates who sit near him. When he becomes frustrated, his peers are either able to help him talk it out, or one will accompany him back to his special education classroom where he can de-stress for a few moments. Sometimes he is able to return to the science class. This happened frequently when he first started going to science, but decreased over time.

John has learned many things from his classmates, including the ability to recognize when he's having difficulty and allowing others to help him. He still has a long way to go, but now has a much better-planned program. Ms. Hart is able to allow for exposure to strong models and provide the intensive academic instruction that she knows John will need for the future. She has hopes of including him more and more as he is able to tolerate it, and the teachers are now understanding that John is on track to be in their classes.

John's IEP team continually monitors his needs in all areas, and the parents are happy to finally see some success with their child's program. Behavior programs also were put into place. They required continual updating, since John's motivators changed. However, the teacher noticed that his choices for motivators were becoming more "typical," in that he was choosing activities or objects that the classmates were also choosing, such as candy bars, soft drinks, more computer time, and the real biggie, no homework for one night.

This helped to lift John's spirits and increased his motivation for written performance. He was also asked to go to a football game with one of the peers. This would never have happened before.

John still has a long way to go, but he is finally seeing some success – the slow-but-steady rate that his teacher has taken has worked well for him. These turbulent times of adolescence finally appear bit brighter for him.

Meet Brendon - Brendon is an upcoming eighth grader. His profile consists of mild autism and moderate cognitive impairment. Although he doesn't typically have any notable behaviors, he has an extremely short attention span for tasks (tons of attention for activities of his own interests, though!), and is on medication for this. He exhibits some self-stim behaviors, such as playing with various aspects of his clothing, but can be directed away from this with one or two verbal or non-verbal cues. Brendon has had the assistance of a full paraprofessional throughout his elementary years, as well as in sixth and seventh grades. He was based in self-contained classrooms for much of his elementary years. He did, though, have some exposure to the typical peers through social programming and peer tutoring. Sometimes this has been conducted in the regular education setting, sometimes within his classroom on a traditional pull-out method, though he was considered an "included student" (admittedly loosely) by both parents and school. Presently, he continues to be below grade level for core academics, but is included in social aspects of social studies, exploratories, homeroom and science. His program to date has been aligned closely to the core academics, hoping that he will be able to understand the concepts better over time. Some he has, but this has not been the case for all.

Brendon's eighth grade IEP requires him to have more instruction in the functional curriculum area, such as functional math and reading, as well as community-based instruction offered for students with moderate intellectual impairment. His parents have agreed to this, since they are now conducting long-term planning for Brendon. Although he will technically be listed as a "self-contained" student since he is receiving three hours of instruction in the MOID classroom, he will also to be viewed as an "inclusion" student philosophically because his teachers all look for ways to include him with the typical peers anywhere and everywhere possible. Because the parents see the years slipping by, they wanted him to access the valuable lessons for community-based instruction with the idea that he will go towards work exploration and apprenticeship work in high school. Community colleges or technical schools will also be considered for selected coursework in the high school years – though that will be a mission for the future. They made their current decisions based on the increased level of social skills that he has demonstrated, and the fact that he continues to require assistance in academics and adaptive skills.

Socially, Brendon has shown dramatic increases over the years. In middle school, he had a formal peer buddy system that allowed him to have buddies for every inclusion class. He attends sporting events and loves the school dances. Brendon is very well-liked by the peers, both typical students and some with disabilities, who "hang" with him at the dances and games, and seek him out at lunch. Brendon has joined an after school club and enjoys the challenge of the games, though they are being vastly modified for him. He also likes to sit and listen to music next to the kids playing on the computer or game.

In eighth grade Brendon's IEP goals will stress increased independence in all areas. He tends toward learned helplessness and taking the easy way out of tasks. This is one reason why the parents want the added instruction in functional math and work skills at this age.

Meet Juanita - Juanita is a very bright young lady in seventh grade. She has a diagnosis of Asperger's Syndrome and was first identified in fourth grade, when her low social skills clearly set her apart from the typical peers, and her level of frustration tolerance seemed far below her age-mates. Juanita's outbursts became more frequent, though not severe. She tended to cry easily and would whine if she felt she was done an injustice (sometimes she was accurate, sometimes not). She has been on routine behavior programs which have helped her to decrease her behaviors and learn more appropriate ways of interacting, though she continues to struggle socially. Currently, Juanita is in a gifted science class. The rest of her schedule is in regular education classes. Juanita's IEP team had a difficult time fitting her profile into the state department of education's definition of autism eligibility. Her parents fought for one segment in resource to address social skills and the team accepted the segment. Although Juanita is very bright, she demonstrates significant social delays. She has been described as "oblivious" when it comes to picking up social or non-verbal cues. As a result, Juanita has been teased through most of her elementary years.

Juanita has had intensive social skills instruction throughout both sixth and seventh grades, which has made it easier for her to defend herself against the teasing. She now knows how to handle the situations much better, and as a result, her peers are backing off. Juanita continues to have times when she is upset and continues on a positive reinforcement system that is coupled with natural consequences. She is having much success in her exploratories, especially band, where the other students fully accept her because of common interests, and in after-school clubs. Another reason that Juanita has had such success with the exploratories is because the teachers have been so receptive to peer programming. At her level, these programs are done more incidentally than overtly. The teachers understand her disability and make sure that she is paired with very receptive peers, plus they have worked out a non-verbal system of cueing which does not call attention to Juanita. Juanita sees herself enjoying school and is looking forward to eighth grade.

Meet Shanita, Jerrell and Franklin - These three students are among a number of other students in a self-contained classroom for students with severe/profound cognitive impairment. Although they are all middle school students, Shanita should have moved on to the high school at the end of this year, but her team decided at the IEP that they would retain her for one more year. Although these three students are ambulatory, three other children in the classroom are not and are in wheelchairs most of the day. Self-help skills, feeding and toilet issues are a major focus of this classroom. Shanita, Jerrell and Franklin's parents are not happy with the total isolation that their children are experiencing and it is the viewpoint of the principal that these students should just "stay out of the way of the normal students." This situation was determined to be unacceptable by the parents who decided to go together to sit down with the principal to talk. Before that, they made a visit (together) to the special education director's office to talk to her about how this program could be changed. Consultants were called in to assess the classroom and recommendations were made as a result of the meeting. They included the following:

- The teacher needed to be reassigned. She had been teaching this same classroom for 5 years and was totally fried. Another teacher was approached and agreed to take the class.
- The new teacher was provided with time to meet with the parents to determine what they wanted for their children.
- Full adaptive behavior, language and social assessments were conducted on all of the students.
- The special education teacher took the consultant's report to the superintendent. She stated that the recommendations were all workable and could be conducted with support from his office. Discussions were held with top administrators as to how to implement many of these recommendations in other schools as well.
- The superintendent had a personal initiative to improve schools, and was excited about innovation coming to the county, reflecting favorably on his system. He asked the special education director to arrange a meeting with the parents.
- The parents met with the superintendent and told him that they, too, were excited about the plans and that they were sure the principal would be too. The superintendent called the principal and determined that he was excited about them, after all!

A meeting was called with the special education director, principal, parents and teacher to outline changes that would be implemented – some right away, some to be worked on. They included:

- An Advisory Board including parents, teachers (regular ed and special ed, related staff), administration, and eventually, a community business person, to establish the mission and then to guide and develop the program over time. Routine, scheduled meetings.

- Formal peer tutor programs – this will set up the mechanism for multitudes of available peer mentors. This will need to be established with the collaboration of DOE and the school system registrar.
- Community-based instruction with typical student mentors, if possible. Parent input as to which community services they want established.
- Attendance at games, dances, etc. Parent volunteers solicited from PTO to help with any details about family transportation to events, though school liabilities must be investigated.
- Assigning of all students to a homeroom class and regular ed teacher regardless of how much time is spent in the class.
- Assigned peers for each student, for each homeroom.
- Lunch-room privileges – including eating in the cafeteria with buddies.
- Continued emphasis on independent functioning skills for eating, toileting, adaptive skills. Much of this will continue to be conducted by the teacher and staff.
- Inclusion of typical peers into the classroom for assistance with some of the adaptive skills, but not all, of course.
- Concurrent P.E. with the typical students in a companion program in the gym - meshing whenever possible.
- Inclusion in numbers of exploratories - including health, art, drama, or other possible courses.
- Credited classes for peer mentors: full portfolio assembled between each student-peer pair.
- Continued emphasis, as always, on individual skills that will mean solid data collection and analysis and adjustment of any portion of the program that is not working, or where lack of progress is shown.

This program will be a solid, well-developed program when all the components are in place and working correctly (author added suggestions to the list that were not included in the original consultant's recommendations - forgive me - author's privilege!). However, this program will not occur overnight. Shanita will see many of the benefits, but probably not all since she will be moving on to high school the next year. This plan, once in place, should provide the skeleton of any program that is designed for a student with severe/profound needs without compromising the needed functional, adaptive and language skills necessary for these students.

A Final Note to Teachers and Parents —

We have been on an adventure in the pages presented here. Please view this book as your start into the world of teaching middle school students with autism/AS. Inclusion with this disability cannot happen overnight, but will never happen if it is not begun with you.

As you can see from the case histories, each student is unique. The inclusion aspect has been well thought out and programmed for success. Yes, for some, the process was started later than with others. Some were more successful than others. But, this is middle school and not elementary school and we are farther down the road to adulthood. However, students with autism/AS can and do learn in the presence of strong models and solid programming. Your efforts will be effective whenever you start them.

Many veteran teachers have stated that inclusion programming was a whirlwind experience that caused them much stress and anxiety, as well as tremendous amounts of time and paperwork. They also found love, enjoyment, and astonishment over learned skills that they never would have believed. They gained their enthusiasm for teaching again, and a real belief that they have increased their professional skills and feel they are better teachers because of the experience. This is not an isolated case, but happens over and over again. Parents and teachers alike are changing lives and changing societies. That has _always_ been our mission in the teaching field, for we never stand still. We are the most creative force on earth. This author hopes that this book will have helped to accomplish this mission in any small portion at all.

Signing off and going to bed. — Sheila Wagner, M.Ed.

REFERENCES

REFERENCES

American Psychiatric Association. (1994). *Diagnostic and Statistical Manual of Mental Disorders* (4th ed.) Wash., D.C. American Psychiatric Association.

Baron-Cohen, S., Allen, J. & Gillberg, C. (1996). Checklist for Autism /PDD in Toddlers. *The British Journal of Psychiatry*, 168, 158-163.

Brady, M. P., Shores, R. E., Gunter, P., McEvoy, M.A., Fox J. J., & White, C. (1984). Generalization of Adolescent's Social Initiation Behavior Via Multiple Peers In A Classroom Setting. *Journal of the Association for Persons with Severe Handicaps, 9,* 278-286.

Brown, L., Schwarz, P., Udvari-Solner, A., Kampschroer, E. E., Johnson, F., Jorgensen, J., and Gruenewald, L. (1991). How Much Time Should Students With Severe Intellectual Disabilities Spend In Regular Education Classrooms And Elsewhere? *The Association for Persons with Severe Handicaps*, 16, 39.

Burrell, B., Wood, S. J., Pikes, T., Holliday, C. (2001). Student Mentors And Proteges Learning Together. *Teaching Exceptional Children*, 33, 3.

Clark, G. (1979). *Career Education For The Handicapped Child In The Elementary Classroom.* Denver, CO: Love.

Clark, G. M., Field, S., Patton, J.R., Brolin, D. E. & Sitlington, P.L. (1994). Life Skills Instruction: A Necessary Component For All Students With Disabilities. A position statement of the Division on Career Development and Transition. *Career Development for Exceptional Individuals*, 17, 125-134.

Deno, S. L., Foegen, A., Robinson, S., Espin, C. (1996). Commentary: Facing The Realities Of Inclusion For Students With Mild Disabilities. *The Journal of Special Education*, 30, 345.

Deschene, C., Ebeling, D. G., Sprague, J. (1994). *Adapting Curriculum & Instruction in Inclusive Classrooms: A Teacher's Desk Reference.* Bloomington, IN: ISDD.

Donnellan, A. M., Mirenda, P., Mesaros, R. A. & Fassbender, L. (1984). A Strategy For Analyzing The Communicative Functions Of Behavior. *Journal of the Association for Persons with Severe Handicaps*, II, 201-212.

Gaylord-Ross, R. J., Haring, T. G., Breen, C., & Pitts-Conway, V. (1984). The Training And Generalization Of Social Interaction Skills With Autistic Youth. *Journal of Applied Behavior Analysis,* 17, 229-247.

Time Timers, Generaction, Inc. Cincinnati, OH.

Gilliam, J.E. (1995). Gilliam Autism Rating Scale (GARS). Wood Dale, IL: Stoelting Co.

Goldstein, A. P., Sprafkin, R. P., Gershaw, N. J., Klein, P. (1980). Skillstreaming the Adolescent: A Structured Learning Approach To Teaching Prosocial Skills. *Champaign, IL: Research Press CO.*

Hammeken, Peggy, A. (1997). *Inclusion: 450 Strategies For Success.* Minnetonka, MN: Peyral Publications.

Huges, C., Eisenman, L. T., Hwang, B., Kim, J., Killian, D. J., and Scott, S. V. (1997). Transition From Secondary Special Education To Adult Life: A Review And Analysis Of Empirical Measures, *Education and Training in Mental Retardation and Developmental Disabilities,* 32, 101.

Kamps, D. M., Leonard, B. R., Vernon, S., Dugan, E. P., and Delquadri, J. C., (1992). Teaching Social Skills To Students With Autism To Increase Peer Interactions In An Integrated First-Grade Classroom. *Journal of Applied Behavior Analysis,* 25, 281-288.

Kaufman, J. M., Hallahan, D.P. (1995). *The Illusion Of Full Inclusion: A Comprehensive Critique Of A Current Special Education Bandwagon.* Austin, TX: PRO-ED, Inc..

Lord, C., & Paul, R. (1997). Language And Communication In Autism. In Cohen, D. J. & Volkmar, F. R. (eds) *Handbook of Autism and Pervasive Developmental Disorders, Second Edition.* New York: John Wiley & Sons.

Malloy, W., Malloy, C. (1997). Deconstructing The Impediments To Responsible Inclusion Through The Essential Schools Option. *Journal for a Just & Caring Education,* 3, 459.

Marks, S. U., Schrader, C., Levine, M. (1999). Paraeducator Experiences In Inclusive Settings: Helping, Hovering, Or Holding Their Own? *Exceptional Children,* 65, 325.

Marks, S.U., Schrader, C., Levine, M., Hagle, C., Longaker, T., Morales, M. & Peters, I. (1999). Social Skills For Social Ills. *Teaching Exceptional Children,* 32, 2.

References

McConnell, M. (1999). Self-Monitoring, Cueing, Recording, And Managing: Teaching Students To Manage Their Own Behavior. *Teaching Exceptional Children*, 32, 2, pp16.

McGee, G. G., Morrier, M. & Daly, T. (1999). An Incidental Teaching Approach To Early Intervention For Toddlers With Autism. *Journal of the Association for People with Severe Handicaps*, 24, 133-146.

McGinnis, E. (1982). An Individualized Curriculum For Children And Youth With Autism. In C.R. Smith, J.P. Grimes & J. J. Freilinger (Eds.), *Autism: Programmatic Considerations* (pp. 170-207). Des Moines, IA: State Department of Public Instruction.

Moore, S. C., Agran, M. & McSweyn, C. A. (1990). Career Education: Are We Starting Early Enough? *Career Development For Exceptional Individuals*, 13, 129-134.

Morreau, L. E. & Bruininks, R. H. (1991). *Checklist Of Adaptive Living Skills* (CALS). Itasca, IL: Riverside Publishing.

Odom, S. L., Hoyson, M., Jamieson, B. & Strain, P. (1985). Increasing Handicapped Preschoolers' Peer Social Interactions: Cross Setting and Component Analysis. *Journal of Applied Behavior Analysis*, 18, 3-16.

Palmer, D.S., Borthwick-Duffy, S. A., Widman, K. (1998). Parent Perceptions Of Inclusive Practices For Their Children With Significant Cognitive Disabilities. *Exceptional Children*, 64, 145-288.

Palmer, D. S., Borthwick-Duffy, S.,A., Widman, K., & Best, S. (1997). *Influences On Parent Perceptions of Inclusive Practices For Their Children With Severe Cognitive Disabilities.* Manuscript submitted for publication.

Prizant, B. M. & Bailey, D. (1992). Facilitating The Acquisition and Use of Communication Skills. In D. Bailey & M. Wolery (Eds.), *Teaching Infants And Preschoolers With Disabilities*. Columbus, OH: Merrill.

Rusch, F.R., DeStefano, L., Chadsey-Rusch, J., Phelps, L.A. & Szymanski, E. (Eds.), (1992). *Transition From School To Adult Life: Models, Linkages, And Policy*. Sycamore, H.: Sycamore.

Scales, P.C. (1991). *A Portrait of Young Adolescents in the 1990's: Implications For Promoting Healthy Growth And Development*. Minneapolis, MN: Search Institute/Center for Early Adolescence.

Schleien, S. J., Mustonen, T. & Rynders, J. E. (1995). Participation Of Children With Autism And Nondisabled Peers In A Cooperatively Structured Community Art Program. *Journal of Autism and Developmental Disorders*, 25, 397-413.

Schopler, E., Reichler, R. J., Renner, B. R. (1988). *The Childhood Autism Rating Scale.* Los Angeles, CA: WPS.

Smith-Myles, B. (2001). Presentation for the ASA-Greater GA. Chapter: Atlanta, GA.

Sparrow, S. S., Balla, D. A. & Cicchetti, D. V. (1984). *Vineland Adaptive Behavior Scales.* Circle Pine, MN: AGS.

Sprague, J., McDonnell, J. (1986). *Effective Use Of Secondary Age Peer Tutors: A Resource Manual For Classroom Teachers.* Bloomington, IN: ISDD.

Voeltz, L. M. (1980). Children's Attitudes Toward Handicapped Peers. *American Journal of Mental Deficiency*, 84, 455-464.

Voeltz, L. M., Hemphill, N. J., Brown, S., Kishi, G, Klein, R., Fruehling, R., Collie, J., Levy, G., & Kue, C. (1983). The Special Friends Program: A Trainer's Manual For Integrated School Settings (rev. ed.). Honolulu, HI: University of Hawaii Department of Education.

Walker, H. M., McConnell, S. R. (1995). Walker-Mcconnell Scales of Social Competence and School Adjustment. Hebron, KY: *Delmar Thomson Learning.*

Wagner, S. (2001). Build Me A Bridge: Successful Transitions Through the School Years. *Autism Digest,* Jan-Feb, pp 10-11.

Wagner, S. (2001). Build Me A Bridge: Successful Transitions Through the School Years, Part II. *Autism Digest,* March-April, pp 26-28.

Wagner, S. (1999). *Inclusive Programming for Elementary Students with Autism.* Arlington, TX: Future Horizons, Inc.

Wigfield, A. & Eccles, J. (1994). Children's Competence Beliefs, Achievement Values, and General Self-Esteem: Change Across Elementary And Middle School. *Journal of Early Adolescence*, 14, 107-138.

Woods, M. (1998). Whose Job Is It Anyway? Educational Roles In Inclusion. *Exceptional Children*, 64, 181.

Appendix

Appendix

Weekly Performance Chart

Student: _____   Grade: _____

Monday 1 - 5	Tuesday 1 -5	Wednesday 1 -5	Thursday 1 -5	Friday 1 -5
Per.1 Teach. Int:				
Per. 2 Teach. Int:				
Per. 3 Teach. Int:				
Per. 4 Teach. Int:				
Per. 5 Teach. Int:				
Per. 6 Teach. Int:				
IEP Holder Summary:				

This graph allows each teacher to grade the student on a scale of 1-5 (teachers can set criteria for the numbered grade), and provide it to the IEP holder at the end of the day. The IEP holder then contacts the parent as needed.

Wagner, S. (2001)

Student Self-Rating

Student: Grade: Date:

Period	Behavior				Amt. Of work			% of participation		Summary
	#1	#2	#3	Sum	a.	b.	c.	Lg grp	Sm grp	
1										
2										
3										
4										
5										
6										

Fig.   Behavior: #1 _____   a. = _____
         Behavior: #2 _____   b. = _____
         Behavior: #3 _____   c. = _____

Parent sig:_____

In this graph, the student rates himself on his behaviors (teachers can set the criteria and the type of scoring - letter grades, point system, etc.), on the amount of work he has completed at set times (a.b.c.) or work tasks, and on his level of participation during large group and small group activities. This form should be taken home each night. Parents can sign and return to the school, or the school can make a copy prior to sending it home.

Wagner, S. (2001)

Daily Phone Log

Student: **Grade:**

Date	Time	Duration of call	Staff	Issues	Resolution	Comments

This graph assists the teacher in documenting contact with the parent. This file should be kept in the student's permanent folder.

Wagner, S. (2001)

Daily Journal

Student: **Grade:**   **Date:**

Class	Participation	Work Performance	Behavior	Summary grade 1 - 5 (5=A)

This graph helps the teacher of each class provide a daily grade for the student in each area, and provides a summary grade for the day.

Wagner, S. (2001)

Daily Check List

Student: **Grade:**

Monday S - 5	Tuesday S - 5	Wednesday S - 5	Thursday S - 5	Friday – Summary
Per.1				
Per. 2				
Per. 3				
Per. 4				
Per. 5				
Per. 6				

Fig.   S= Satisfactory; 1 = F; 2= D; 3= C; 4 = B; 5 = A

This graph allows the teacher to quickly rate the student for each period and provide a summary for Friday. The student can take this form home each night, or wait until Friday. Teachers should put their initials in each box, as well as the grade.

Wagner, S. (2001)

Student Performance Chart

Student Name: _____ Date: _____ Teacher initials: _____

Class: _____ Did: _____well _____not well _____ %participated

Homework turned in: _____yes _____no   appropriate behaviors _____yes _____no
Comments:

Student Name: _____ Date: _____ Teacher initials: _____

Class: _____ Did: _____well _____not well _____ %participated

Homework turned in: _____yes _____no   appropriate behaviors _____yes _____no
Comments:

Student Name: _____ Date: _____ Teacher initials: _____

Class: _____ Did: _____well _____not well _____ %participated

Homework turned in: _____yes _____no   appropriate behaviors _____yes _____no
Comments:

Student Name: _____ Date: _____ Teacher initials: _____

Class: _____ Did: _____well _____not well _____ %participated

Homework turned in: _____yes _____no   appropriate behaviors _____yes _____no
Comments:

Student Name: _____ Date: _____ Teacher initials: _____

Class: _____ Did: _____well _____not well _____ %participated

Homework turned in: _____yes _____no   appropriate behaviors _____yes _____no
Comments:

Wagner, S. (2001)

Parent Letter

Dear Parents,

(Student's name) has been selected to participate in a special program designed to assist students with disabilities in your school. This program will provide assistance to students with social skills needs.

(Student's name) was identified and selected by a team of teachers because of his/her skills and abilities, his/her ease with fellow classmates, and his/her warm, caring and outgoing personality.

In order for (student's name) to participate in this program, we must have your permission. He/she will be paired with a disabled student during portions of the day to act as a model of strong social skills. He/she will also help this student interact socially with other students. He/she may be asked to sit alongside the student at lunch time to talk and introduce them to others. She/he may also help them transition from class to class, invite them to after-school activities on occasion, and generally help pave the way, socially, for a student in need. No academic time will be compromised for your student, nor should their academic grades be affected at all.

This program strictly targets social skills and we hope (student's name) will form a strong bond with the student with whom they have been paired, and that this student will learn appropriate social behaviour from your child.

Peer tutoring is a long-standing program to teach better and more appropriate skills to students with disabilities. We hope that you will allow your child to participate in this worthy program and that they, too, will learn from the experience.

Please complete the bottom portion of this letter and return it to your child's homeroom teacher. We thank you for your consideration of this program and would be happy to answer any questions that you may have. We can be reached at:_____.

Student's Name: _____

Grade _____ *Homeroom Teacher:* _____

Parent's Name: _____

Address: _____

Phone Number: _____   _____

I give my permission for my child to be a peer tutor: _____Yes _____ No

Parent Signature/Date: _____

Teacher Collaboration Form

WHEN CAN YOU MEET?

Teacher:_____   Student:_____

_____M	_____3:00	List of Concerns:
_____T	_____3:15	_____
_____W	_____3:30	_____
_____Th	_____3:45	_____
_____F	_____4:00	_____
Week of	_____4:15	(Return to Ms. Jones)

Teacher Collaboration Form

WHEN CAN YOU MEET?

Teacher:_____   Student:_____

_____M	_____3:00	List of Concerns:
_____T	_____3:15	_____
_____W	_____3:30	_____
_____Th	_____3:45	_____
_____F	_____4:00	_____
Week of	_____4:15	(Return to Ms. Jones)

Wagner, S. (2001)

BEHAVIOR RECORDING FOR MEDICATION MONITORING

Student Name: _____ DOB: _____ Grade: _____

Parents: _____

Physician: _____ Phone # _____ Fax # _____

School: _____

Day of: _____ Week of: _____

Enter the targeted behaviors (one per line) for the particular student. Please circle the appropriate number for the listed behavior based on observation for the day or week desired. Provide this information to the parent, or fax to the doctor to aid in medication monitoring.

	None		Medium		High	
1. _____	0	1	2	3	4	5
2. _____	0	1	2	3	4	5
3. _____	0	1	2	3	4	5
4. _____	0	1	2	3	4	5
5. _____	0	1	2	3	4	5
6. _____	0	1	2	3	4	5
7. _____	0	1	2	3	4	5
8. _____	0	1	2	3	4	5
9. _____	0	1	2	3	4	5
10. _____	0	1	2	3	4	5

Comments/Narrative:

_____   _____   _____
Teacher Signature   Date   Faxed?

Wagner, S. (2001)

EVALUATION FORM FOR INCLUSIVE PROGRAM

This form is offered to teachers and parents to evaluate the middle school student's inclusive program.

Evaluation Procedure:

1. Each team member should receive an evaluation form to complete at the end of each semester.

2. Upon completion, each member should present their input to the team members at the Treatment Team Meeting.

3. Based on the information provided by team members, brainstorming techniques should allow for improved programming.

Criteria	Areas met:	Areas of concern:	Projected action/change:
1. Access to regular education students			
2. Social initiations/ responses			
3. Behavior Plan - Developing Appropriate skills			
4. Appropriate Language with Peers			
5. Academic gains			
6. Therapies: OT			
7. Therapies: Speech			

MOTIVATIONAL SURVEY
ON-GOING ANALYSIS

This form is intended to assist the classroom teacher or paraprofessional in providing information on student preferences for behavior programming. On-going observations should be conducted on the individual child in a variety of settings, to record opinions that the child has towards certain objects or activities. Place a check in the appropriate box according to how the individual feels towards that particular item. This information can then be used in conjunction with positive behavioral practices in the classroom, and for building a portfolio on the student. Any object or activity that is recorded in the "Much" or "Very much" column can likely be used as a reinforcer for task learning.

Student Name: _____

(The Student Likes . . .)

Date	Item (Objects, Activities, etc.)	Neutral	Not at all	Some	Much	Very Much

Wagner, S. (2001)

TRANSITIONING STUDENTS WITH AUTISM/AS
PORTFOLIO INFORMATION
Emory Autism Resource Center

Student Name:_____ DOB: _____

School Leaving:_____ Going to: _____

Last Teacher:_____ Future Teacher:_____

Date of Portfolio: _____ This portfolio covers dates: _____ to _____

Parents Name/Address: _____

_____

Section I: General Description of the student:

• Physical: (Gross motor, fine motor, physical agility, etc.)

• Personality:

Section II: • Social (please include the following):
  _____ Current social skills assessment (Walker-McConnell; Skillstreaming, etc.)
  _____ Skills mastered this past school year

Description of student's overall social skills:

Section III: • Language (please include the following):
  _____Assessments conducted in the past school term

Description of child's language (Give examples of statements the student makes routinely; provide examples of beginning of last year as compared to the present):
  _____Verbal language
  _____ Non-verbal language
  _____ Pragmatic language

Language continued:

<u>**Section IV:**</u>   • Behavior (please include any of the following that are applicable):
_____ Behavior Plan
_____ Reinforcement survey
_____ Examples of behavior forms
_____ Data collection sheets
_____ Functional Analysis of Behavior/results
_____ Reactive Plan

Description of routine behaviors by student (please describe an ordinary day and what you see):

Behaviors that are seen rarely, but are of significant levels to be of concern:

Behaviors continued:

Behaviors which may pose safety issues:

Other Behavior issues:

Section V: • Academic (please include the following):
___ Examples of math computation
___ Examples of reading level
___ Examples of handwriting
___ Report card
___ Examples of tests

Academics continued:

Describe the student's areas of strength and areas of challenge academically.

Identify routine modifications that are made for this student, and include examples, if possible.

Section VI: • Adaptive Behaviors (please include the following, if applicable):
_____ Vineland Adaptive Behavior Scales - Classroom Version
_____ Any other checklists that address adaptive behaviors
_____ Toileting information
_____ Eating information
_____ Sensory information
_____ Other daily/routine functioning

Section VII: Please include into this portfolio any other examples that may be of importance to the next school teacher, so that they may have a better idea of what this particular student is like.

Other necessary information:

Wagner, S. (2001)

Class Materials List

Date:_____   Day: _____

Class	Which book is needed?	Got your note-book?	Turned in Assign?	Got pen? Sharp pencil?	Stored other books?	Got extra paper?	What's tonight's assign?	Pts earned
Per. 1								
Per. 2								
Per. 3								
Per. 4								
Per. 5								
Per. 6								

Check off each box or award points: 0-5

The above graph can be reduced to fit a 3X5 card or smaller, if necessary. The number of points that the student awards himself for completing each segment can be a prior decision between student and IEP holder and can change over time.

Wagner, S. (2001)

BEHAVIOR TRACKING FORM

STUDENT NAME: _____ DOB: _____ CLASSROOM: _____ TEACHER: _____

Date/Time	People involved/ Activity	Antecedent/ Triggering event	Description of Behavior	Duration/How long did it last?	Consequence/ Others' responses	Comments

Wagner, S. (7/99 EARC)

RESOURCES

Resources for Successful Inclusion Programs - K-12:

Although this is a middle school book, teachers often change grade levels, crossing age-levels. Therefore, resources are offered for K-12 to investigate and share.

BOOKS:

Adapting Curriculum & Instruction in Inclusive Classrooms: A Staff Development Kit, 2nd Ed.
Author(s): S. Cole, B. Horvath, C. Chapman, C. Deschenes, D. G. Ebeling, and J. Sprague
To Order Contact:
Indiana University at (812) 855-9396
http://www.isdd.indiana.edu/~cedir/public.html

Adapting Curriculum & Instruction in Inclusive Classrooms: A Teacher's Desk Reference, 2nd Ed.
Author(s): S. Cole, B. Horvath, C. Chapman, C. Deschenes, D. G. Ebeling, and J. Sprague
To Order Contact:
Indiana University at (812) 855-9396
http://www.isdd.indiana.edu/~cedir/public.html

Adapting Curriculum & Instruction in Inclusive Classrooms: Video
To Order Contact:
The Forum on Education
812-855-5090 (phone)
812-855-8545 (fax)
http://www.isdd.indiana.edu/~cedir/public.html

Asperger's Huh?: A Child's Perspective
Author(s): Rosina G. Schnurr, Ph.D
To Order Contact:
Future Horizons, Inc.
721 W. Abram Street
Arlington, TX 76013
800-489-0727
Fax: 817-277-2270
www.FutureHorizons-autism.com
ISBN: 0-9684473-0-9

Asperger Syndrome and Difficult Moments
Author(s): Brenda Smith Myles, Jack Southwick
To Order Contact:
Future Horizons, Inc.
721 W. Abram Street
Arlington, TX 76013
800-489-0727
Fax: 817-277-2270
www.FutureHorizons-autism.com
ISBN: 0-96725140-0

Blue Bottle Mystery: An Asperger Adventure
Author: Kathy Hoopmann
To Order Contact:
Jessica Kingsley Publishers
116 Pentonville Rd
London N1 9JB
www.jkp.com
ISBN: 1-84310-007-X

Connecting Students: A Guide to Thoughtful Friendship Facilitation for Educators & Families
Author(s): C. Beth Schaffner, Barbara E. Buswell
To Order Contact:
PEAK Parent Center, Inc.
6055 Lehman Drive, Suite 101
Colorado Springs, CO 80918
(719) 531-9400

Creating Inclusive Classrooms: Effective and Reflective Practices
Author(s): Spencer J. Salend
To Order Contact:
http://www.amazon.com
ISBN: 0-13-019073-X

Deciding What to Teach and How to Teach It: Connecting Students Through Curriculum and Instruction
Author(s): Elizabeth Castagnera, Douglas Fisher, Karen Rodifer, Caren Sax
To Order Contact:
PEAK Parent Center, Inc.
6055 Lehman Drive, Suite 101
Colorado Springs, Colorado 80918
(719) 531-9400

Helping the Child Who Doesn't Fit In
Authors: Stephen Nowicki, Jr., Ph.D. and Marshall P. Duke, Ph.D.
To Order Contact:
Peachtree Publishers
494 Armour Circle, N.E.
Atlanta, Georgia 30324
ISBN: 1-56145-025-1

How to be a Para Pro: A Comprehensive Training Manual for Paraprofessionals
Author(s): Diane Twachtman-Cullen
To Order Contact:
Future Horizons, Inc.
721 W. Abram Street
Arlington, TX 76013
800-489-0727
Fax: 817-277-2270
www.FutureHorizons-autism.com
ISBN: 0-9666-5291-6

How to Differentiate Instruction in Mixed-Ability Classrooms
Author(s): Carol Ann Tomlinson
To Order Contact:
Association for Supervision and Curriculum Development (ASCD)
Alexandria, Virginia
www.ascd.org
1-800-933-2723
ISBN: 0-87120-245-X

How to Handle Bullies, Teasers and Other Meanies: A Book that takes the Nuisance
Out of Name Calling and Other Nonsense
Author(s): Kate Cohen-Posey
To Order Contact:
Rainbow Books or your local book seller

Inclusion: 450 Strategies for Success
Author(s): Peggy A. Hammenken
To Order Contact:
Peytral Publications
PO Box 1162
Minnetonka, MN 55345
Tel: 612-949-8707
Fax: 612-906-9777
ISBN: 0-9644271-7-6

Inclusion: A Guide for Educators
Author(s): Susan Stainback & William Stainback
To Order Contact:
Paul H. Brookes Publishing Co.
P.O. Box 10624 Baltimore, Maryland 21285-0624
www.brookespublishing.com
ISBN 1-55766-231-2

Inclusion: A Teacher's Guide
Author(s): Susan Craig, Ann G. Haggart
To Order Contact:
AGH Associates, Inc.
Box 130
Hampton, NH 03842
603-926-1316

Inclusion Strategies for Students with Learning and Behavior Problems: Perspectives, Experiences, and Best Practices
Edited by: Paul Zionts
To Order Contact:
Pro-Ed, Inc.
8700 Shoal Creek Boulevard
Austin, Texas 78757-6897
ISBN: 0-89079-698-X

Inclusive High Schools: Learning from Contemporary Classrooms
Author(s): Douglas Fisher, Caren Sax, Ian Pumpian
To Order Contact:
Paul H. Brookes Publishing Co.
P.O. Box 10624
Baltimore, Maryland 21285-0624
www.brookespublishing.com
ISBN: 1-55766-379-3

Inclusive Middle Schools
Author: Craig H. Kennedy & Douglas Fisher
To Order Contact:
Paul H. Brookes Publishing Co.
P.O. Box 10624
Baltimore, Maryland 21285-0624
www.brookespublishing.com
ISBN: 1-55766-486-2

Inclusive Programming For Elementary Students with Autism
Author(s): Sheila Wagner
To Order Contact:
Future Horizons, Inc.
721 W. Abram Street
Arlington, TX 76013
800-489-0727
Fax: 817-277-2270
www.FutureHorizons-autism.com
ISBN: 1-885477-54-6

Incorporating Social Goals in the Classroom: A Guide for Teachers and Parents of Children with High-Functioning Autism and Asperger Syndrome
Author(s): Rebecca A. Moyes
To Order Contact:
Future Horizons, Inc.
721 W. Abram Street
Arlington, TX 76013
800-489-0727
Fax: 817-277-2270
www.FutureHorizons-autism.com
ISBN: 1-85302-967-X

Inside Out: What Makes a Person with Social Cognitive Deficits Tick?
Author(s): Michelle Garcia Winner
To Order Contact:
Future Horizons, Inc.
721 W. Abram Street
Arlington, TX 76013
800-489-0727
Fax: 817-277-2270
www.FutureHorizons-autism.com
or visit: http://www.socialthinking.com
ISBN: 0-9701320-0-X

Lesson Plans and Modifications for Inclusion and Collaborative Classrooms
Author(s): The Master Teacher, Inc.
To Order Contact:
National Professional Resources, Inc.
25 South Regent Street
Port Chester, NY 10573
TEL: 1-800-453-7461
FAX: 1-914-937-9327
http://www.nprinc.com

Lessons for Inclusion
Authors: Terri Vandercook, Rebecca Rice Tetlle, Jo Montle, June Downing, Jackie Levin, Martl Glanville,
Barbara Solberg, Sherri Branham, Linda Ellson, Donna McNear
To Order Contact:
Institute on Community Integration (UAP)
109 Pattee Hall, 150 Pillsbury Drive SE, Minneapolis, MN 55455
(612) 624-4512

Making It Work On Monday
Author(s): Susan L. Fister, Karen A. Kemp
To Order Contact:
Sopris West Educational Services
4093 Specialty Place
Longmont, CO 80504
(303) 651-2829
http://www.sopriswest.com

Making School Inclusion Work: A Guide to Everyday Practices
Author(s): Katie, Blenk, Doris Landau Fine
To Order Contact:
Brookline Books
P.O. Box 1046
Cambridge, MA 02238-1046
ISBN 0-914797-96-4

Negotiating the Special Education Maze: A Guide for Parents and Teachers, 3rd ed.
Author(s): Winifred Anderson, Stephen Chitwood, Deidre Hayden
To Order Contact:
Woodbine House, Inc.
6510 Bells Mill Rd.
Bethesda, MD 20817
(800) 843-7323
ISBN: 0-933149-72-7

Of Mine and Aliens: An Asperger Adventure
Author: Kathy Hoopmann
To Order Contact:
Jessica Kingsley Publishers
116 Pentonville Rd
London N1 0JB
www.jkp.com
ISBN: 1 85302 978 5

Reach Them All: Adapting Curriculum & Instruction with Technology in Inclusive Classrooms.
Author(s): M. Hounshell, M. Irwin, S. Ely, S. Soto, M.B. Janes, and V. Morrison
To Order Contact:
Indiana University at (812) 855-9396
http://www.isdd.indiana.edu/~cedir/public.html

Skillstreaming for the Adolescent: A Structured Learning Approach to Teaching Prosocial Skills
Author(s): Arnold P. Goldstein, Robert P. Sprafkin, N. Jane Gershaw, Paul Klein
To Order Contact:
Research Press Company
2612 North Mattis Avenue
Champaign, Illinois 61821

Skillstreaming the Elementary School Child: A Guide for Teaching Prosocial Skills
Author(s): Ellen McGinnis & Arnold Goldstein with Robert P. Sprafkin & N. Jane Gershaw
To Order Contact:
Research Press Company
2612 North Mattis Avenue
Champaign, Illinois 61821

Teaching Children with Autism: Strategies to Enhance Communication and Socialization
Author(s): Kathleen Ann Quill
To Order Contact:
Delmar Publishers, Inc.
Box 15015 3 Columbia Circle
Albany, NY 12212-5015
http://www.delmar.com/delmar.html
ISBN: 0-8273-6269-2

The Explosive Child
Author(s): Ross W. Greene
To Order Contact:
Harper Collins Publishers
10 East 53rd Street
New York, NY 10022
ISBN: 0-06-017534-6

The New Social Story Book – Illustrated Edition
Author(s): Carol Gray
To Order Contact:
Future Horizons, Inc.
721 W. Abram Street
Arlington, TX 76013
800-489-0727
Fax: 817-277-2270
www.FutureHorizons-autism.com
ISBN: 1-88547-766-X

The Tough Kid: Social Skills Book
Author(s): Susan M. Sheridan, Ph.D., Part of the "Tough Kid" Series by Rhode, Jenson, & Reavis
To Order Contact:
Sopris West Educational Services
4093 Specialty Place
Longmont, CO 80504
(303) 651-2829
www.sopriswest.com
ISBN: 1-57035-051-5

Together We Can!: ClassWide Peer Tutoring to Improve Basic Academic Skills
Author(s): Charles R. Greenwood, Joseph C. Delquadri, Judith J. Carta
To Order Contact:
Sopris West
4093 Specialty Place
Longmont, CO 80504
(303) 651-2829
http://www.sopriswest.com
ISBN: 1-57035-125-2

Writing Social Stories with Carol Gray
Video workshop with accompanying handout booklet
Available From:
Future Horizons, Inc.
721 W. Abram Street
Arlington, TX 76013
Video: $99.95
800-489-0727
Fax: 817-277-2270
http://www.FutureHorizons-autism.com

No cost publications:

U.S. Department of Education, Education Publication Center: Call or log onto this web site to request a variety of free publications offered through the U.S. Department of Education including *A Guide to the Individualized Education Program* which walks you through the IEP process step by step.

Education Publication Center
U.S. Department of Education
P.O. Box 1398
Jessup, Maryland 20794-1398
Toll Free: (877) 4ED-Pubs (433-7827)
Toll Free TTY/TDD: (877) 576-7734
Fax: (301) 470-1244
E-mail: edpubs@inet.ed.gov
On-Line ordering: http://www.ed.gov/pubs/edpubs.html

Implementing IDEA: A Guide for Principals
This publication can be downloaded in PDF format from
http://www.ideapractices.org/principalsguide.htm
or you can call toll free to order a hard copy.
1-877-CEC-IDEA

Journals/Magazines/Newsletters:

Autism/Asperger's Digest
For Subscription Inquiries Contact:
Future Horizons, Inc
721 W Abram Street
Arlington, TX 76013
800-489-0727
Fax: 817-277-2270
www.futurehorizons-autism.com

Education and Training in Mental Retardation and Developmental Disabilities
For Subscription Inquires Contact:
The Journal of the Division on Mental Retardation and Developmental Disabilities
The Council for Exceptional Children
1110 North Glebe Rd.
Arlington, VA 22201

Journal of Autism and Developmental Disorders
For Subscription Inquiries Contact:
Plenum Publishing Corporation
233 Spring Street
New York, N.Y. 10013
(212) 620-8468, -8470, -8472, -8082

Teacher Education and Special Education
The Journal of the Teacher Education Division of The Council for Exceptional Children
For Subscription Information Contact:
Division of Teacher Education
College of Education
PO Box 210002
University of Cincinnati
Cincinnati, OH 45221-0002
(513) 556-4552
http://www.tese.uc.edu

Exceptional Children
The Council for Exceptional Children (CEC)'s special education research journal
For Subscription Information Contact:
1920 Association Drive
Reston, BA 20191-1589
1-888-232-7733
http://www.cec.sped.org

Advocate
The Newsletter of the Autism Society of America (requires membership to ASA)
For Subscription/Membership Information Contact:
Autism Society of America
7910 Woodmont Avenue
Suite 650
Bethesda, MD 20814
http://www.autism-society.org/

The Source
A Publication of Asperger Syndrome Coalition of the United States, Inc. (requires membership to ASC)
For Subscription/Membership Information Contact:
ASC-U.S., Inc.
P.O. Box 49267
Jacksonville Beach, FL 32240-9267

Websites to Visit:

http://www.asa.org
This is the web-site for the Autism Society of America. Here you can find a plethora of information as well as links to each state's local chapters of the Autism Society.

http://www.feat.org
Families for Early Autism Treatment

http://www.asperger.org
Asperger Syndrome Coalition of the U.S.

http://www.udel.edu/bkirby/asperger.org
Online Asperger Syndrome Information and Support (O.A.S.I.S)

http://www.cureautismnow.org
Cure Autism Now (CAN) Official Website

http://www.autism.com
The Autism Research Institute

http://www.autism-pdd.net
Autism-PDD Resources Network

http://www.futurehorizons-autism.com
Future Horizons, Inc., the world leader in quality autism/Asperger's Syndrome publications. They publish and sell many books which deal with understanding autism/Asperger's Syndrome, as well books intended for professionals and paraprofessionals who are educating or training children and adults with autism/Asperger's Syndrome.

http://www.naar.org
The National Alliance for Autism Research

http://members.tripod.com/~transmil/alp.htm
The Autism Link Page—Check here for links to every site imaginable!

http://www.autismconnect.org
A worldwide forum for sharing of information by people whose lives are touched by Autism.

http://www.egroups.com/group/GA
A Parent Network for parents/guardians of school-aged children with disabilities in the state of Georgia.

http://www.isn.net/~jypsy/
The official Website of "Oops . . . Wrong Planet!" This site includes Information and Links on Autism.

http://www.autism.org/
Center for the Study of Autism

http://www.aspergers.com
This is an Asperger's Syndrome Homepage from the University of Massachusetts Medical Center.